CULTURE SHOCK!
Mexico

Mark Cramer

Graphic Arts Center Publishing Company
Portland, Oregon

In the same series

Australia	Hong Kong	Singapore	London at Your Door
Bolivia	India	South Africa	Paris at Your Door
Borneo	Indonesia	Spain	Rome at Your Door
Britain	Ireland	Sri Lanka	
Burma	Israel	Sweden	A Globe-Trotter's Guide
California	Italy	Switzerland	A Parent's Guide
Canada	Japan	Syria	A Student's Guide
Chile	Korea	Taiwan	A Traveller's Medical Guide
China	Laos	Thailand	A Wife's Guide
Cuba	Malaysia	Turkey	Living and Working Abroad
Czech	Mauritius	UAE	Working Holidays Abroad
Republic	Morocco	USA	
Denmark	Nepal	USA—The	
Egypt	Netherlands	South	
France	Norway	Vietnam	
Germany	Pakistan		
Greece	Philippines		

Illustrations by TRIGG

© 1998 Times Editions Pte Ltd
Reprinted 1998

This book is published by special
arrangement with Times Editions Pte Ltd
Times Centre, 1 New Industrial Road, Singapore 536196
International Standard Book Number 1-55868-399-2
Library of Congress Catalog Number 97-074477
Graphic Arts Center Publishing Company
P.O. Box 10306 • Portland, Oregon 97296-0306 • (503) 226-2402

Printed in Singapore

In memory of Julien Maller
who gave us great joy in his short life
and immense sorrow in his death.

An ancient sculpture recalls Mexico's long, rich history.

CONTENTS

Acknowledgments   7

Map of Mexico   8

Introduction   9

1 Social Setting   14
2 Physical Setting   39
3 Profiles   52
4 Social and Business Customs   99
5 Mexican Adventures   140
6 Mexico in Crisis   163
7 Survival Skills   170

Strategic Directory   199
Cultural Quiz   210
Further Reading   218
The Author   220
Index   221

ACKNOWLEDGEMENTS

For photographs: Juan Carlos Vega Camacho, Bolivian architect who visited Mexico (phone: 591-2-363813), Carlos Mendoza, Berni Peredo, Tátiana Percero with the Mexican Government Tourism Office, Mike Carr, and Doug Aberley.

For interviews and insights: Maya Lorena Pérez Ruiz, anthropologist, Dr. José María Muriá, historian, Luis Gómez, journalist, General Nicolás Fernández, the Chamula gentleman whose name I do not recall, Peter Berg, Kozo Nakahara, and hundreds of other people who helped me along the way.

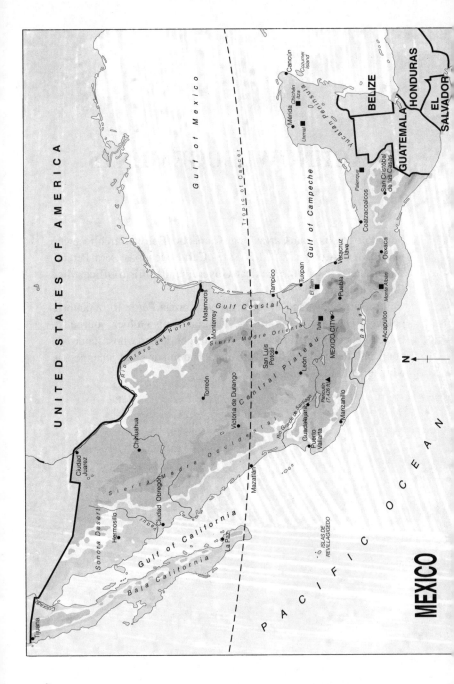

UNITED STATES OF AMERICA

Gulf of Mexico

Tropic of Cancer

Tijuana

Sonora Desert

Hermosillo

Ciudad Juarez

Chihuahua

Ciudad Obregón

Sierra Madre Occidental

Mazatlán

La Paz

Gulf of California

Baja California

Torreón

Victoria de Durango

Central Plateau

Sierra Madre Oriental

San Luis Potosí

León

Guadalajara

Puerto Vallarta

Paricutín
(7,267 ft)

MEXICO CITY

Tula

Manzanillo

Acapulco

Río Bravo del Norte

Matamoros

Monterrey

Tampico

Tuxpan

El Tajín

Puebla

Veracruz Llave

Balsas

Oaxaca

Monte Albán

Coatzacoalcos

Palenque

San Cristóbal
de las Casas

Gulf of Campeche

Gulf Coastal

Río Grande de Santiago

ISLAS DE
REVILLAGIGEDO

PACIFIC OCEAN

N

Cancún

Cozumel
Island

Mérida

Chichén
Itzá

Uxmal

Yucatán Peninsula

BELIZE

GUATEMALA

HONDURAS

EL SALVADOR

MEXICO

8

INTRODUCTION

AVOIDING THE TRAP

An international stereotype industry has flourished for a half century thanks to its primary product: the Mexican. A typical Mexican figure in sculpture or painting adorning restaurants and hotels is the *agachado*. He is seated on the ground in the shade of an enormous *sombrero* that resembles a giant mushroom. He is taking a *siesta*.

Complementing this rural image is the urban stereotype of the *pelado*, a lumpenproletariat rebel without cause. He rises from a table strewn with empty bottles of Corona Beer and amidst moans of melancholy, incites social disturbance, referred to as *relajo*.

Never mind that the *agachado* is simply taking a break from a twelve-hour work day in the fields, or that the *relajo* caused by the *pelado* pales in comparison to the acts of British hooligans or American fraternity pranksters.

Then there is the image of *mañana*. The Mexican arrives late or puts off tasks because he has little regard for life. *La vida no vale nada* (life is worth nothing) says the soulful ranchera song. Why confront life when you must confront death at every turn?

Resulting from such stereotypes are comments (or bad jokes) like those of Chicago columnist Mike Royko: "Mexico is a useless country. And before its entire population sneaks across the border, we should seize it and make it a colony."

If the international tourism industry inadvertently adds fuel to these inflaming stereotypes, Mexico's own well-meaning intelligentsia, allied with a more opportunistic popular culture industry, promotes Mexican caricatures that remarkably resemble the foreign-made product.

Mexican-Catalán author Roger Bartra observes "curious parallels between old books of racist and colonialist heritage" and "*la filosofía de lo mexicano*" that emerged within Mexico following the Revolution of 1910.

In his *The Cage of Melancholy: Identity and Metamorphosis of the Mexican*, Bartra traces the bookish roots of Mexican stereotypes from the works of intellectuals like José Vasconcelos, Samuel Ramos, and Nobel Prize winning Octavio Paz, to the products of popular culture such as the films of Cantinflas.

Bartra theorizes that the distorting but unifying force of this mythological national culture has served the interests of the State.

"A spectacle is created of the people themselves, so that they may purge themselves of tribulations, frustrations and sins," in a type of national catharsis, an invention of national culture that ensures subservience to the sociopolitical system.

One example: the romanticizing of Mexico City tenement life in various Pedro Infante films. There is a fluffy stylizing of the gruesome details of hunger, violence, promiscuity and unsanitary conditions of Mexico City *vecindades* (tenements).

Another example: an old black and white Cantinflas movie. A military leader must tape a radio address to inspire patriotism during wartime. Cantinflas works for the leader. Playing around with the recording device, Cantinflas produces his own recording, using popular language and confusing demagoguery. The two recordings get switched and Cantinflas's version is aired on the radio the next day. Upon hearing that his speech has been substituted, the military leader is furious. As he is about to strangle Cantinflas, a phone call arrives from headquarters; the public has been overwhelmed by patriotic fervor thanks to the speech. Cantinflas is instantly forgiven by his boss. Both the military leader and Cantinflas receive promotions. Popular culture, as represented by the lingua Cantinflesca, has served the rulers in their quest for the backing of the people.

Bartra alleges that "myths" have been fomented by various Mexican intellectuals. José Vasconcelos developed his "cosmic race" theory. Rejecting the "cold" Anglo-Saxon and Nordic cultures, Vasconcelos lauded the more exuberant Mexican culture that emerged from the combination of the indigenous and Spaniard bloods: the *mestizo*.

In appearance, Vasconcelos had presented a positive view of the Mexican, but it was nonetheless racially-based and catered to stereotypes of the past, especially those conjured up by nineteenth century "positivist" thinkers.

Once the revolution had solidified into a ruling party in 1929, along came Samuel Ramos with his *El perfil del hombre y la cultura en México* in the mid-thirties, in which he affirmed that the machismo of the *pelado* was the result of a national inferiority complex.

Nobel Prize winner Octavio Paz reworked Ramos's ideas in his 1959 *The Labyrinth of Solitude*. Now, the inferiority complex is given historical roots. The Mexican is the product of an historical and literal rape. Conquistador Hernán Cortés creates the first mestizo in Mexico, Martín, out of the union with his indigenous mistress and translator, Marina, referred to by Mexicans as *La Malinche*.

Today the word *malinchista* is synonymous with "traitor." The mother of all Mexicans is perceived, inaccurately, as a traitor. And the father of all Mexicans is a rapist. The result is an inferiority complex, an internal conflict in which part of the Mexican (the indigenous) hates the other part of the same Mexican (the Spaniard), the latter labeled pejoratively as the *gachupín*. It has taken Mexico much longer than other Latin American countries to reconcile itself with its Spanish colonial past.

The result of these mythical-historical contradictions, according to these philosophers of the Mexican character, is that the Mexican hides behind a psychological mask, unmasking himself once a year in a frenetic fiesta, and then returning to his pathological seclusion. (We shall examine the imagery of masks in a section on popular culture at the end of Chapter Three.)

Octavio Paz is essentially a poet, and many of the eloquent ideas in this and his subsequent essay *Posdata* are so exquisitely spellbinding in their poetic elaboration, that the reader pardons the shortage of objective evidence.

These writings contain a trap for the first-time visitor to Mexico, who may arrive with a built-in prejudice based on a literal interpretation of what has been written by Vasconcelos, Ramos, and Paz. Or the visitor may have internalized what has been seen in the superbly entertaining films of Cantinflas and Pedro Infante.

Such would be the equivalent of visiting the United States and expecting to find the world of Woody Allen in New York or the Raymond Chandler *noir* in the brilliant light of Southern California.

A menacing trap for the newcomer to Mexico would be to resort to facile stereotypes that create insurmountable barriers between visitors and their Mexican hosts.

The cultural barrier between foreigner and Mexican is further complicated by Mexico's cultural diversity; more than 50 ethnic groups and corresponding languages have survived nearly five centuries of blatant or subtle attempts at cultural annihilation or assimilation.

For many years, modern Mexico, in the absence of a functional cultural map, groped for roads to assimilation, with the generic word *campesino* (peasant) replacing words like Indian or indigenous. The historical Indian was cherished in the Museum of Anthropology but the contemporary Indian was ignored.

Professor Miguel León-Portilla never yielded in his efforts to recover endangered cultures until in 1996 he proudly wrote that "The indigenous word, the ancient one, is in the process of rescue." Much of the credit for the resurgence of cultural diversity is attributed to the beloved anthropologist Guillermo Bonfil Batalla. In his *Mexico Profundo* (Profound Mexico), Bonfil pierced through the outer tiers of Mexican existence, in search of living reverberations of Mexico's heritage, beyond what he labeled "imaginary Mexico".

Bonfil suggests that getting to know Mexico in an intimate way is not at all a simplistic or stereotypical exercise.

"Today's expressions of our civilization are very diverse:" he wrote, "from those cultures that some Indian communities have been able to conserve with a great degree of internal cohesion, to the great quantity of isolated traits distributed in a different way in distinct urban sectors."

The approach here, then, must be open-ended. We shall avoid placing rigid frames around cultural traits. Instead, we shall introduce a wide variety of Mexican characters, observing how they respond to dramatic settings. We will not shy away from way-of-life patterns, but in the end, the reader will be left with a profusion of anecdotes, testimonies, hard data, and strategic information.

I hope that the Mexicans who emerge in this book will transcend the prototypical recreations found in much of the travel literature about Mexico.

SOCIAL SETTING

The indigenous Americas are the product of ancient migrations from Asia over the Bering Straight. The Spaniards were not the first to invade indigenous Mexico. The Chichimecas, warrior nomads, arrived in various waves from the north. In the 14th century, the last wave, today known as the Aztecs, settled in the valley of Mexico, stopping there, according to legend, when they saw an eagle standing on a cactus eating a snake. This prophecy is now an image on the Mexican flag. The Aztec empire would spread as far south as Honduras.

The nomads would adapt to the ways of preceding cultures like the Mayans, Zapotecs, Olmecs, and the enigmatic Toltecs, incorporating agriculture, urban centers, art, and writing. From those previous theocracies, the Aztecs adopted human sacrifice in order to appease the bloodthirsty Gods.

The influence of social reformer-turned-god Quetzalcoatl (plumed serpent) failed to eclipse the more demanding and cruel Gods: Tlaloc, the rain God, and Tezcatlipoca (Smoking Mirror). These dieties were incorporated from previous cultures, but Huizilopochtli, who craved human hearts, was an Aztec creation.

Quetzalcoatl, the humane antithesis of these cruel Gods, was expected to return from the east, roughly around 1519, which coincided with the arrival of the crafty Spanish *conquistador* Hernán Cortés.

The Aztecs inhabited the great canal city of Tenochtitlán. Today what is left of these canals can be seen in Xochimilco, on the southern outskirts of Mexico City.

The Spanish conquest may be understood as one imperialism challenging another. The Aztecs, rather than occupy their conquered territories, sent in collectors of tributes, a system the Spaniards would later co-opt for their own purposes.

Much of Aztec culture was derived from the Mayans, with their complex writing, calendar, and pyramids in the south, the Zapotecs of Monte Albán in Oaxaca, the Olmecs, with their frightening, stone-sculpted Olmec heads, and the grand Toltec city of Tula, whose pottery and temples influenced Native American cultures from Costa Rica to Illinois. Aztec nobility would claim to be descended from the Toltec.

Even the great pyramids of the central valley north of Mexico City belonged to another culture: Teotihuacán, the largest pre-conquest empire, with nearly a quarter of a million inhabitants, whose Pyramid of the Sun was constructed only a century or two after the time of Jesus Christ. Teotihuacán's urban planners and agricultural scientists dominated for several centuries until the culture turned imperialistic and like all empires, became fractured from both without and within.

THE CONQUEST

Chronicles from the period portray a vacillating Aztec emperor Moctezuma, reluctant to resist Cortés; the bearded Spaniard was perceived as the returning god Quetzalcoatl (*Kulkulcán* to the Mayas). Some versions picture the Aztecs as intimidated by the Spaniards' horses, which made the *conquistadores* look like giant fearful animals.

15

More strategic in the conquest may have been devastating European diseases such as smallpox, against which the Native Americans had no natural resistance.

Another significant factor working in favor of the invading Europeans was an indigenous hatred toward the imperialistic Aztecs. Cultures under the Aztec dominion not only paid demanding tributes but saw the hearts of their defeated warriors torn out by Aztec priests to placate the Gods. These colonized cultures were ready and willing to ally themselves with Hernán Cortés against a common enemy.

The small Spanish band should have been intimidated by Tenochtitlán, larger than European cities of the time. Conquistador Bernal Díaz del Castillo chronicles his amazement at avenues wider than anything known in Europe.

The Spaniards were first received as visitors by Moctezuma. But when Cortés had abandoned the city to confront political opposition arriving from Spain, the less-astute Spaniard caretakers he had left

Photo: Carlos Mendoza

Xochimilco, vestige of the extensive system of canals in the great city of Tenochtitlán.

behind, fearing imminent Aztec attacks, engaged in a pre-emptive strike and were routed in what has become known as *La Noche Triste* (The Sad Night). The more gold a fleeing Spaniard hauled away, the more likely he'd sink in the city's canals, turning them a brilliant red.

Cortés returned to Tenochtitlán with less than a thousand men, but accompanied by 100,000 disenfranchised anti-Aztec natives, especially Tlascaltecs, as well as portable boats to confront the Aztec canoes. After house-to-house, building-to-building battles, the Aztecs succumbed. With Moctezuma dead (it's not certain whether at the hands of the Spaniards or his own people), the 18-year-old emperor Cuauhtémoc asked Cortés to finish him off, but Hernán Cortés refused to do so. Mexican histories elaborate that Cuauhtémoc was later tortured.

(Today, the leading figure in one of Mexico's opposition political parties bears the name Cuauhtémoc, as does a member of Mexico's national football-soccer team.)

For an engaging account of the conquest, read Bernal Díaz del Castillo, *Historia verdadera de la conquista de la Nueva España*, available in English language translation.

17

One pre-Hispanic culture, the P'urhépechas (also known as Tarascans) of Michoacán to the west of Mexico City, successfully resisted Aztec imperialism, as corroborated through linguistic evidence. Throughout Mexico, names of cities and towns have the typical Aztec ending *tlán* from the Nahuatl tongue, but locations in Michoacán end with *átzcuaro* from the P'urhépecha.

CULTURE SHOCK FROM WITHIN

In the realm of sheer drama and bizarre personalities, few histories can rival Mexico's, and indeed, Mexico today is a country where history remains unrelentingly alive, as contrasted with its neighbor to the north, where the idiomatic expression "that's history" means it's dead and no longer of relevance.

Having traveled in eleven Latin American countries, I am struck by the totally unique view that Mexico takes of the Conquest. In other Latin American countries, one does not hear of the good guys and the bad guys in this event, for today's inhabitants are the racial and cultural combination of those two confronting cultures.

But in Mexico, the good guys were the native Americans. Cuauhtémoc is the hero and Cortés is the villain. When Mexicans express hatred for a conniving, villainous Cortés, they are expressing antagonism against part of themselves. The Nahuatl word for the conqueror, *gachupín*, is still used pejoratively against the Spaniard, and derived from that word is *gacho*, which exists only in Mexican Spanish and means ugly.

One particular Mexican joke will help us grasp this intrinsic culture clash.

In 1937, a Mexican goes to Spain to fight in the Spanish Civil War, on the side of the Republicans. In battle, he is captured by the fascists. He begs for his life, promising the fascists that he will fight valiantly on their side against the Republicans.

The fascists grant him the opportunity, and the Mexican proves to be a fierce warrior, killing many Republicans.

"How can you do it?" asks a fascist companion. "A few days ago you fought on the side of the Republicans. Now you are killing them? Don't you have values?"

"Sure I do," responds the Mexican. "I came here to kill *gachupines*."

(This joke satirizes an irrational, historical hatred of Spaniards. Historically, the Mexican intelligentsia sided in words and deeds with the Spanish Republicans, and Republicans, in turn, were received with open arms as refugees in Mexico.)

But the intrinsic culture clash remains a living historical myth. One of the disenfranchised Native Americans who opposed the imperialistic Aztecs was the woman who would become Cortés's mistress and able translator, Marina. Historians believe that Marina's translations aided the Spanish conquest. Known as *La Malinche*, she would later be maligned by popular historians as a traitor, and her brilliant attributes would be officially understated.

Another arm of the conquest was the Catholic clergy. The legalistic Spaniards needed a rationale in order to willingly conquer another people. Gold was not considered a legitimate moral rationale. But religion was. The priests drew up lists of sins of the Indians, one of which was that they engaged in the pagan custom of bathing regularly.

Conquering Spaniards were required to read the reasons for the conquest to the tribes who were about to be subdued. One of the more reflective *conquistadores* wrote sarcastically about the ritual of reading reasons to people who did not understand the language. The only way to enable the Spaniards to undertake this noble task in a fair manner, he reasoned, would be to kidnap a native, teach him Castilian, and then bring him back to his tribe to translate the reasons for conquest.

THE COLONIAL PERIOD

Unable to uproot indigenous religions, the priests superimposed one religion upon another; each indigenous saint and festival was bestowed a Catholic equivalent. Today's Mexican Catholicism is a legacy of this religious fusion.

European diseases altered the complexion of the colonial period in its initial stages. By 1548, a scant two decades and a half after the arrival of Cortés, such a large portion of the indigenous population had been decimated by European diseases that Africans imported to fill the labor void outnumbered Indians in the valley of Mexico.

The pillar of the colonial system was the *encomienda*. Conquering warriors and later colonizers were granted *encomiendas*: rights to labor and tributes from groups of Indians in a particular region/ terrain. In turn, the colonizers were required to convert the natives to Catholicism, but the system was a rationale for slavery.

Some but not all Spaniards participating in the Conquest were criminals and low-lifes who saw in the Americas a means to acquire nobility. Manual labor was undignified for the Spanish nobleman; in the Americas Spaniards were treated to a large and earnest labor force.

A typical leitmotif in Spanish literature from the classic medieval Picaresque novel *Lazarillo de Tormes* to the nineteenth century novels of Galdós, involves a down-and-out nobleman who has lost his fortune. In order to maintain appearances, the nobleman avoids telltale physical labor. His faithful servant goes out to do odd jobs, providing for his master.

In the construction of Mexico's superb colonial cathedrals, it was Indian labor that climbed the scaffolds and carved the stone of the baroque facades. Spanish baroque churches thus become mestizo works of art; Indian artisans, left to their own resources high on the scaffolds, would fashion indigenous imagery to accompany the figures that the idle Spaniard below had commissioned.

The colonial period would last for nearly three hundred years. Curiously, conquistadors, priests and later colonizers sustained the medieval version of Catholicism that had been altered back in Europe by the impact of the Reformation.

Medieval culture traits placed regional and ideological constraints on the colonial economy. Mexico and other parts of Spanish America functioned as producers of raw materials for Spain and

Photo: Juan Carlos Vega

The cathedral in Morelia: an example of Mexican Baroque.

nothing more, and the Spain of the Inquisition, late to adopt capitalism and modern banking systems, in turn became a subcolony of the rest of Europe. Spain functioned as a sieve through which the wealth of its colonies poured into other European countries.

The masterful baroque, convent poetry of Sor Juana Inés de la Cruz documents how the colonial culture thwarted personal development of a *criollo* woman. (*Criollo* means Spaniard born in the Americas.) The best of Mexican colonial literature was written by a woman whose anguish allowed her to transcend the literary mannerisms of baroque times.

Treatment of Indians and Africans remained inhumane. A few colonial reformers attempted to reduce the harsh exploitation so as to not deplete the human capital required to sustain the colony. Other reformers were the equivalent of today's human rights advocates, especially the Dominican Friar Bartolomé de las Casas.

Traditional histories allege that Las Casas had supported the importation of blacks to alleviate the condition of the Indians, but recent investigations by the eminent historian Silvio Zavala (*Por la senda hispana de la libertad*, 1993) suggest that Fray Bartolomé de Las Casas soon "repented," in his own words *"porque la misma razón es dellos que de los indios"* (because they [the blacks] have the same rights as the Indians).

The native Spaniard was considered superior to the *criollo,* who was relegated to the second tier of a complex caste system. Although of the same race as Spaniards, criollos were described in some original Spanish documents as inferior because of the air they breathed in the Americas. What would the writers of such documents say about today's foul ocher air in the Valley of Mexico?

INDEPENDENCE

Father Hidalgo's "Grito de Dolores" marked the onset of the war of independence on September 16 of 1810. Hidalgo and his colleague Morelos (a mulatto), were priests imbued in the Enlightenment. The indigenous soldiers in their movement were perceived by the criollo elite as unruly hordes.

Eventually, the criollos, under Iturbide, wrested control of the independence movement from the Indian-loving priests. Hidalgo and Morelos were both executed, and independence in 1821 became a simple change of power from Spaniards born in Spain to Spaniards born in the Americas, under Emperor Agustín de Iturbide.

Iturbide would be deposed by 1823, replaced by a republic that remained under the total control of the criollos. Economic relationships between the dominant landowning class and the laboring Indians hardly changed.

In order to divide mestizos from Indians, the criollos pushed the ideology that the mestizos' Spanish blood made them superior. Mestizos were often employed as go-betweens and *capataces*, foremen and enforcers of order against the indigenous masses.

Mexico was to pass through a typical post-independence period of political anarchy, with an economy constrained by former colonial models. A symbol of the period was Antonio de Santa Anna, eleven times president of Mexico. General Santa Anna left the presidency several times to fight wars in 1836 and 1848 against Texas and the United States. On other occasions, he abandoned the presidency to enjoy his fighting cocks on his *hacienda* in Veracruz. Yet on other occasions he was exiled by the wrath of the people for his extravagance, corruption, and failed military adventures, once escaping death in his pyjamas.

Santa Anna's interpreter during the General's exile in Staten Island, New York, was a man named Adams. Adams noticed that Santa Anna would chew on a bitter substance. Adams added sugar and flavors, creating the Adams Chewing Gum Company. The brand name "Chicklets" came from the Aztec word *chicle*.

Although Santa Anna bore some degree of personal responsibility for Mexico's loss of Texas, California and other valuable territories, even the most disciplined Mexican army would not have resisted the U.S. ideology of Manifest Destiny.

The underlying cause of the Mexico's defeat was her anachronistic colonial economy. Three hundred years of colonialism had left the country without the type of national entrepreneurial class capable of establishing economic footholds in distant regions.

At the opposite extreme of Mexico to the south, the War of the Castes in Yucatán saw the Mayan Indians wrest control from time to time from the criollo landlords. (See Nelson Reed's classic, *The Caste War of Yucatán*, Stanford University Press, 1964.) The tenacious Mayans were eventually defeated. Today's Zapatista movement is in some ways a reincarnation of caste wars. In Mexico, history periodically unburies itself and resurfaces with a new face.

LA REFORMA

The war of *La Reforma* (1858-1861) nudged Mexico ever so slowly into the modern capitalistic era. Reformer Benito Juárez, a full-blooded Zapotec Indian, first needed to expel the French invaders, who had occupied Mexico through their puppet Austrian prince Maximiliano under the guise of collecting debts. The classic black and white American movie, *Juárez*, starring Paul Muni, is the tragic story of the downfall of the naive Maximiliano and his devoted but increasingly deranged wife, Carlota.

General Zaragoza's 1862 defeat of the French led to what is today celebrated as *Cinco de Mayo*.

With the French in retreat, Maximiliano was left by Napoleon III to fend for himself. Carlota made desperate trips to Europe, pleading for military support of her besieged husband.

Benito Juárez knew that Maximiliano had been a mere puppet, and he may have even sympathized with the plight of the prince. But for symbolic reasons of national sovereignty, Juárez had Maximiliano executed at Cerro de las Campanas in Querétaro in 1867.

Today, Maximiliano's castle stands as an impressive museum in the heart of Mexico City's vast Chapultepec forest.

As Juárez's liberal economics attempted to implant capitalism in Mexico, he unintentionally disenfranchised his indigenous countrymen. Prior to La Reforma (now the name of a glorious, tree-lined boulevard in Mexico City), the Indians worked their collective lands called *ejidos*. But as an institution, the collective ejido did not mesh with principals of liberal individualism.

As ejidos were broken up, *hacendado* landowners absorbed the liberated lands, thus expanding their power. But the short-sightedness of colonial economics inhibited them from converting their vast holdings into thriving capitalistic enterprises, as Juárez would have wished.

Another Juárez creation, *Los Rurales*, was a rural police force intended to protect trade routes, but eventually became an arm of a post-Juárez police state.

A comrade of Juárez in the wars of La Reforma, Genera' Porfirio Díaz, became an elected dictator for more than three decades, under the banner of "Order and Progress." A modernizing Mexico eased slowly into the economic sphere of the United States and other foreign powers, leaving the indigenous and mestizo masses in misery. It was commonplace for hacendados and their sons to rape the wives of Indian farm laborers, and slavery returned to several forlorn regions of Mexico. (See John Kenneth Turner's *Barbarous Mexico*.) Los Rurales ran rampant over the countryside, inspiring more fear and hatred than the bandits they opposed.

The *hacendados* operated virtual feudal kingdoms. Luis Terrazas owned 14,000 square kilometers alone in Chihuahua. Farm workers owed their soul to the company store, and once in debt, were required to remain on the hacienda until all debt was paid off. Debt was passed on to offspring.

One debt slave in Chihuahua was a young man named Doroteo Arango, whose sister was raped by the hacendado's son. Arango escaped, resurfacing as the legendary bandit, Pancho Villa. The rebel's mentor was a progressive democratic landowner, Francisco I. Madero, who transformed Villa into a revolutionary.

LA REVOLUCIÓN

In 1910, Madero, an unlikely insurgent with his short build and high-pitched voice, initiated a revolution that surged far beyond his control. Madero envisioned that democratic elections would solve Mexico's problems, failing to grasp the need for a restructuring of the economy.

Emiliano Zapata in Morelos and Francisco "Pancho" Villa in the north, both peasants, would lead revolutions to overthrow the hacendados. Madero was swept into the presidency by the successes of Villa and Zapata. His 1911 election was a mere formality. With no signs that Madero would be willing to restructure land tenure, his former allies Zapata (under the banner of "Land and Liberty") and Villa resumed the bloody revolution.

The aristocracy expected Madero to defend its interests. When he lost control of his former allies, conservatives, including one of Madero's own ministers Victoriano Huerta, engineered an urban coup in 1913, labeled "La Decena Trágica", in which thousands of civilians died. U.S. Ambassador Henry Lane Wilson, antagonistic to Madero, unabashedly supported Huerta. Madero and his unfortunate vice-president Pino Suárez, were executed. Between bouts of sever alcoholism, Huerta attempted to rule Mexico with an iron fist.

Although personalities and ideologies differ, parallels to the 1973 coup against Salvador Allende in Chile are remarkable. Both Allende and Madero were propelled to the elected presidency by more militant factions, and both believed naively that an entrenched plutocracy would cede power peacefully. Both trusted their scheming military leaders. During their regimes, both were hounded by supporters craving radical reform. Both Chile's Augusto Pinochet and Mexico's Huerta were generals who grabbed power through massive urban repression and the support of the American Embassy, and both employed extra-legal brutality to subdue sympathizers of the previous regime.

Sixty years after the fall of Madero, Allende could have learned from the mistakes of his Mexican counterpart. With the death of Madero, Zapata and Villa were back in action.

Much has been written about the "lack of ideology" of Villa and Zapata, whose movements were grounded in concrete and immediate reality. A more ideological but much less effective wing of the Mexican Revolution was led by the anarchosyndicalist Ricardo Flores Magón.

Villa and Zapata, like the insurgent priests exactly a century earlier, were backed by throngs of oppressed peasants. Fearing a total overhaul of the status quo, more moderate factions within Mexico supported two other "constitutionalist" revolutionaries, Venustiano Carranza in Coahuila, and Alvaro Obregón in Sonora.

Following the 1914 defeat of the plundering Huerta, the Zapatistas and Villistas would be obligated to confront new enemies: their former allies Carranza and Obregón.

The lack of political savvy and pronounced regionalism on the part of Zapata and Villa frustrated their alliance after the two had entered Mexico City triumphantly in 1915 and symbolically shared the presidential seat. Neither the populist Villa nor the land-reformer Zapata thirsted for national power.

All the while in Morelos, the Zapatistas enacted spontaneous land reform. In 1919, Carranza coaxed Zapata to a meeting in Chinameca. Against the advice of his followers, Zapata went to the designated spot in an hacienda courtyard, where he was gunned down.

At one point, Villa had captured "El Perfumado" Obregón, but failed to execute him. President Wilson's arms embargo was clearly one-sided, with the Carranza-Obregón faction easily securing arms while the Villistas were left with nothing. The desperate Villistas lost the crucial Battle of Celaya to Obregón in 1915.

Why did Pancho Villa invade Columbus, New Mexico in 1916? One Villista oldtimer, Lauro Trevizo, once interviewed by this author as part of an historical research project, insisted that the raid on Columbus was motivated by President Wilson's arms embargo. Villa had been purchasing arms at Columbus, according to Trevizo, and in the last arms shipment, "there were bullets that exploded without flying out of the rifles. That's why we attacked Columbus."

Carranza became president of Mexico in 1917, drafting a new constitution, but beyond the paperwork, little was done to alleviate rural poverty. The fighting continued until 1920, and Carranza was chased out of office by Obregón.

Between 1920 and 1924, under the administration of Obregón, a national reconstruction program oversaw the building of rural schools, and Obregon's education minister, José Vasconcelos, of *Raza Cósmica* fame, helped forge a new national mythology. The most obvious part of the Vasconcelos program was the contracting of ideological mural painters to adorn the insides and outsides of public buildings.

Diego Rivera, José Alfaro Siqueiros, José Clemente Orozco, and other great mural painters created various styles that would extend beyond the borders of Mexico. Orozco became disenchanted with the demagogic designs of the regime and turned out both murals and paintings depicting the suffering of a people on a more universal

Photo: Juan Carlos Vega

Mural by Juan Chávez Morado, with library mural in the background, National Autonomous University of Mexico, Mexico City.

plane. Later muralists like Rufino Tamayo would embrace cultural rather than political themes.

These and other talented muralists of the Mexican Revolution prove that art can be both highly sophisticated and yet reach and move the uneducated. The historical consciousness created by the mural painters cannot be underestimated, and today, Mexican mural art is revered throughout the world.

Francisco Villa attempted to live a peaceful rural life near Durango but was shot down in 1923 during the regime of the man he had once pardoned, Obregón. Obregón met a similar fate in 1928. During such turbulent times, to die by a bullet was a "natural death".

THE CRISTEROS: CULTURE CLASH II

The centuries-old rift between Spaniard and Indian is but one of Mexico's intrinsic culture clashes. When Plutarco Elías Calles succeeded Obregón in 1924, he became the most radical proponent of a second profound culture conflict.

Like all Latin American nations, Mexico is predominantly Catholic. The Church had supported the aristocracy from the colonial period through the Porfirio Díaz dictatorship.

Although the two insurgent leaders of the 1810 independence movement were priests, both fathers Hidalgo and Morelos had been scorned by the Church hierarchy. One hundred years later, the hacendados attempting to put down the revolution were blessed once more by the church hierarchy.

A thread of anticlerical sentiment was woven into a full-fledged war in which Calles decided once and for all to shut out the influence of the Church. Considering Mexico's vast baroque traditions, Calles was fighting against impressive historical imagery.

Calles closed Church-run schools and convents, deported foreign clerics, prohibited outward displays of religion, and even banned traditional processions. The Cristeros fought back in what is known as the Cristero Rebellion. Many of the Cristeros needed no prodding from Church hierarchy; they were ordinary folk whose culture was under siege.

The rebellion ended in 1929, but not before an anticlerical policy was firmly entrenched. For many subsequent decades, it was a no-no for a Mexican president to attend mass, and priests and nuns could not wear their religious garb in public. Once again, Mexico was split by a type of culture rift unheard of in other Latin American countries.

(During a social function at a Mexican embassy, I mentioned to the Cultural Attaché that a new guest had arrived, a Mexican priest who had done exciting anthropological work. "We're not interested in him," responded the Attaché. "According to the Mexican constitution, priests are second-class citizens, and that's the way it should be.")

But religious festivals continued to adorn the human landscape in post-Calles Mexico. The theology of liberation in the 1960s and 70s along with the reforms of Pope John XXIII little by little restored the honor of the Catholic Church in the eyes of those who had gone astray.

THE PRI

What is today known as the Partido Revolucionario Institucional was forged by Calles in 1929. His legacy would last uninterrupted for nearly seven decades, as Mexico lapsed into one-party rule with ritual elections in which an opposition party, the right-center PAN (Partido Acción Nacional), would receive a few electoral bones. As the century evolved, the Mexican people became increasingly disenchanted with the corruption and demagoguery of their dominant party. The PRI was propped up by the Azcárraga family, owners of the Mexican TV monopoly called Televisa.

As a student in the 70s, I witnessed incidents of severe government repression only to return home and watch TV news reports with no reference to such events.

The government owned the paper companies, and newspapers too daring in their criticism might find themselves with no paper to print

the news. On one occasion, when Mexico's *Excelsior* was becoming too rebellious, the PRI engineered a coup d'etat, purging the paper of many of its greatest intellectuals. A nucleus of these writers moved on to form the prestigious weekly magazine *Proceso*. More than a few cases of murdered journalists further darkened the horizon for those who advocate freedom of expression.

The Mexican comedian Palillo, himself jailed on occasions for his acerbic critiques, was ignored by the PRI-dominated TV stations but still operated out of tents and small clubs. One of his jokes will illustrate the issue of freedom of press under the PRI.

A Gringo and a Mexican were having drinks in a bar. The Gringo bragged, "In my country, we have freedom of expression."

"So do we," garbled his Mexican companion.

"But in my country," countered the Gringo, "we can stand in front of the White House and yell *Death to Nixon*, and nothing will happend to us."

"Big deal," retorted the Mexican. "Here in Mexico, we too can stand in front of our White House, *Los Pinos*, and we too can shout *Death to Nixon*, and I assure you that nothing will happen to us either."

Televisa support of the PRI was echoed by Mexico's eternal labor boss, Fidel Velásquez, known as "el estorbo de México" (Mexico's

obstacle) by labor activists. Velásquez molded a corporatist confederation of workers' unions, called *sindicatos charros* (cowboy unions) by Velásquez detractors. When a legitimate strike materialized,
Velásquez cohorts would send in goons to stifle the dissent.

(As Mexican democracy opened up during the regime of Ernesto
Zedillo, the twin promotional pillars of the PRI, Emilio Azcárraga and
Fidel Velásquez, would pass away in 1997, the latter at the age of 97.)

In the countryside, the institution of *La Torta* was a PRI mainstay.
A torta, in Mexico, is a sandwich on a French-type bread with meat,
jalapeño peppers, avocado, beans, onion and tomato.

Campesinos would be trucked to election sites, given their torta by
PRI officials, and then asked to vote.

The typical Mexican medium for expression of discontent is the
satirical joke:

When PRI padrino Carlos Hank González was running for the
governorship of the State of Mexico, he appeared at a political rally
in the countryside.

The PRI moderator lifted his arms and prodded the crowd to chant:
"Viva Hank González."

The crowd shouted:
"Viva Juan González."

The frustrated moderator chided the crowd.
"No, it's *Viva HANK González.*"

The crowd shouted, again:
"Viva Juan González!"

The now furious moderator asked, "Why can't you just say *Viva
HANK González?*"

Finally, one of the campesinos raised his hand and responded:
"What do you expect? That for just a *torta* we're going to learn
English?"

Throughout the PRI reign, the Mexican sense of humor served as
a compensating device for the lack of free expression. Most notably,
Rius's popular and now classic comic books, *Los Supermachos* and

later *Los Agachados*, would not only satirize the PRI but would belittle aspects of the "national culture" that the PRI manipulated to assure its support.

Lázaro Cárdenas

The PRI, today referred to as "the dinosaurs" even by some reform-minded members from within, was born of revolution and certain vestiges of Mexican social consciousness were maintained by the party to protect its own reputation. These included the Agrarian Reform and nationalization of the oil industry.

Typical social reforms were either initiated or substantially improved during the regime of Lázaro Cárdenas (1934-40). Land distribution was escalated, with a redesigned form of the ancient *ejido* system (peasant cooperatives) as the dominant model of Cárdenas land reform.

Following the Cárdenas period, most of Mexico's arable land was distributed to peasants. In the early eighties, one *ejidatario* in the dusty highlands of Chihuahua told this writer that "my plot of land has already been distributed five times. But there is no water here so I'm thinking of abandoning it and going somewhere else."

Author Juan Rulfo's classic story, "They Gave Us the Land," narrates from a *campesino* perspective a trek into a scorched promised land, a grim legacy not intended by the revered Cárdenas.

In response to popular demands, Cárdenas nationalized foreign oil holdings into Petroleos Mexicanos (PEMEX) in 1938. This dramatic story is narrated in B. Traven's novel, later made into a classic Mexican film, *The White Rose*.

Lázaro Cárdenas was unique among PRI leaders in making the types of bold social moves that the Mexican Revolution would have applauded. But he also institutionalized many of the top-heavy structures that would inhibit even the most reform-minded PRI members.

During his regime, the system of *caciques*, regional strongmen loyal to the central government, was solidified. In the name of labor

33

rights, the centralized Confederación de Trabajadores Mexicanos would later develop into an arm of the State under Fidel Velásquez. In the Calles tradition, Cárdenas continued the PRI custom called *El Dedazo* (roughly "the big pointed finger") by naming his successor.

FOREIGN RELATIONS

Throughout this portrayal of Mexican history and social philosophy, the distinctiveness of Mexico relative to other Latin American countries has been highlighted. In the realm of foreign policy, the Mexican tradition of non-intervention met its greatest test when the United States, through the Organization of American States, called for a trade embargo against Cuba in the early sixties. Mexico was the only Latin American member state to defy the U.S., continuing trade and tourism contracts with the island ruled by Fidel Castro.

The Tlatelolco Massacre

A milestone in Mexican history during the late-sixties was the massive university and high school student movement. Single-party rule, police corruption, government control of the media, and spending for the imminent 1968 Olympic Games, were all factors that led to the dramatic student revolt. The movement peaked when more than a half million people, led by students but including laborers and middle class sympathizers, demonstrated in Mexico City's central plaza, the Zócalo, on August 27.

On October 2, the Plaza of the Three Cultures (with ancient indigenous ruins, colonial structures and modern apartment buildings) became the scene of a peaceful evening vigil.

Suddenly, a rain of bullets pelted the defenseless protesters. Witnesses insist that the attack originated from both sharpshooters in tall buildings overlooking the plaza and from helicopters above.

President Díaz-Ordaz and Interior Minister Luis Echeverría (the next president) were widely blamed for ordering the attack, whose goal was to insure the celebration of the 1968 Olympics.

Versions differ as to how many hundreds of people were thus sacrificed to meet this goal.

(Tlatelolco would suffer another convulsion 17 years later when a great earthquake devastated the apartment complex.)

As the next president, Echeverría ushered in an *"apertura democrática"* ("democratic opening"). By switching just two letters, cynical Mexicans called it the "apretura democrática" ("democratic squeeze"). Protests in the early 1970s were disrupted violently by an obscure group called the Falcons (*Los Halcones*). In reaction, guerilla groups led by rural school teachers Lucio Cabañas and Genaro Vásquez, sprung up in the mountains of the State of Guerrero. Mexican insurgency had evolved according to the times. Two priests led the charge in 1810. In 1910, they were two peasants. And in the 1970s, they were two school teachers.

Both teacher insurgents were eventually gunned down by government troops. But the myth of progress under one-party rule had dissipated forever. Two primary reactions were prevalent: one of cynicism and withdrawal, the other of social activism. Emerging was an independent press and a political coalition that would eventually be capable of challenging the PRI.

In 1988, it was generally believed that Cuauhtémoc Cárdenas, of the two-party left-center National Democratic Front coalition had won the presidential election. But during the vote count, what *Newsweek* called a mysterious collapse of the computation system left Cárdenas as the loser to the PRI's Carlos Salinas de Gortari.

President Salinas de Gortari, applauded by administrations in the United States, would usher in a period of neoliberal economics that culminated in the North American Free Trade Agreement between Mexico, the United States, and Canada.

Contemporary Mexico has been under a siege of drug trafficking violence, devaluations of the peso approximately every six years, increasing crime in the cities, and a film industry that was resorting to cheap sex and violence, a far cry from Mexico's great classic era of cinema.

Some of this violence was generated by divisions within the PRI itself, culminating in the assassination of PRI presidential candidate Luis Donaldo Colosio.

THE ZAPATISTAS

On New Years Day, 1994, the day NAFTA would take effect, Mexico and the world were stunned. History lives on in Mexico, and from the jungles and mountains of the strikingly beautiful State of Chiapas, an armed insurrection emerged, primarily of indigenous origin, but with the masked and pipe-smoking Subcomandante Marcos as the movement's primary spokesperson.

So overtly oppressive was the near feudal control of landowners and political bosses (*caciques*) in Chiapas, that public opinion within Mexico and abroad obligated the Mexican government to negotiate with the Zapatistas in an on-and-off stalemate. From within Chiapas, the Zapatistas received moral support from sectors of the clergy. Later in 1994, the opposition PRD (Partido de la Revolución Democrática) claimed to have been robbed of the governorship by the PRI and declared a parallel state government, supporting the activist villagers who evicted PRI officials from regional government offices.

From beyond the borders of Mexico, human rights activists, pro-indigenous advocates, and other Zapatista sympathizers have been lured by Chiapas and the tourist industry of San Cristóbal de las Casas has received an inconceivable boost.

Meanwhile, from within the PRI, an old guard member, former president Salinas's brother Raúl, was arrested for the murder of a leading reformist member, Francisco Ruiz Massieu. More than a hundred opposition activists were murdered during the Salinas regime, and a discredited Salinas fled the country like so many other Mexican ex-presidents.

As these turbulent events transpired, on the streets of Mexico, not much had changed. Tourism continued to thrive, and poorer Mexicans invented new and creative ways for survival.

Accompanying an increase in crime and cynicism was a renaissance in the arts, in film, literature and painting.

The results of the July 6, 1997 elections represented a profound democratic opening, with the PRI failing to win a majority in congress for the first time in its nearly seven decades of domination. Tenacious PRD's Cuauhtémoc Cárdenas, son of Lázaro Cárdenas, was elected to the newly-created office of governor of the Federal District (D.F.), which includes the sprawling Mexico City. An opposition party is thus holding the second most powerful position in Mexican politics.

Credit for the profound transformation may be attributed to the resolve of Mexican people of all ideologies, the economic crisis, the Zapatistas, or president Zedillo himself. Zedillo, a Mexican Gorbachev, appointed a true independent, the great intellectual José Woldenberg, to preside over the Electoral Institute, thereby assuring the defeat of his own party. (In prior elections, the PRI itself directed the Electoral Institute.)

What Zedillo surrendered in power, he may have gained back in prestige. The free elections won back a sector of citizens who previously saw in the Zapatistas the only alternative. But subsequent paramilitary killings of Zapatista sympathisers, including women and children, suggest that the PRI elite in Chiapas will resort to the most drastic measures to protect its dominant position. Support for the Zapatistas only increased after a 1998 PRI-supported massacre of 35 Indian villagers which saw Zedillo's reformist image tarnished.

Such a detailed historical introduction is not usually imperative for this type of book. But Mexicans are intensely conscious of their history. Zapata is murdered; new Zapatistas emerge nearly eighty years later. The emperor Cuauhtémoc is tortured to death; a new Cuauhtémoc arises a half millenium later. Your awareness of Mexican history and its continuing influence will serve as an essential if not vital bridge in both social and business relations with the people of this exciting land.

Unless you are traveling to the Lacandón jungle of Chiapas (Zapatista land) or riding on crowded buses with wads of dollars in unprotected pockets, Mexico remains a truly magnificent place to visit. *Culture Shock! Mexico* will open avenues for interaction with these most hospitable and engaging people.

– Chapter Two –

PHYSICAL SETTING

When my Salvadoran friend René was nabbed outside a bus station by Mexican immigration authories, he had no document that would permit him to be legally in Mexico. He had swum across a river that separated Guatemala from the southern state of Chiapas, and had hitched north to the highlands of Puebla. His ultimate goal: to find work in the United States.

René faced certain deportation. His only tool of defense was his considerable verbal agility. But how could he disguise his Salvadoran accent, a quicker and more aspirated version of the Spanish language than that found in the central highlands of Mexico? Back in El Salvador, they "swallow" final syllables, especially those ending in the letter s.

But René knew his human geography. He knew that throughout Latin America, the tropical, lowland versions of Spanish had much in common, while the slower highland speech patterns enunciated each and every consonant. He knew that the Spanish of Mexico's coastal regions and lowland jungles was much more akin to his Salvadoran version.

"You're not from here, are you," the agent asked sternly.

René could not affirm that he was from Puebla, a city he knew little about. On the other hand, he knew that the *Jarochos* from the tropics of Veracruz spoke with a tropical drawl similar to his own.

"No señor," he responded. "Yo soy Jarocho!"

Foreigners are not supposed to know that the nickname for a Veracruzano is "Jarocho." The man with the totebag must be telling the truth.

"Está bien," said the immigration officer.

René's knowledge of Mexican regionalism had gotten him out of a jam. (Days later, in Mexico City, the *Jarocho* would talk his way into an ID card and gig from the dominant PRI party, and then vote five times in the presidential election.)

Rene's arduous and intermittent voyage through the length of Mexico began in the southern mountains, which, after San Cristóbal de las Casas, plunged into tropics between Tuxtla-Gutiérrez and the Straight of Tehuantepec. René took a break from the heat on a funky Tehuantepec beach at Salina Cruz on the Pacific coast, before ascending once again to the cooler climes of Oaxaca, and later Puebla.

He would stop off in Mexico City, where supposedly only half the citizenry of working age was fully employed.

"Here, I find jobs everywhere," René applauded. He was comparing Mexico City with San Salvador.

He first worked for General Motors as a mechanic, until he found refuge with the PRI.

Following the elections, the PRI gig dried up. René continued his trek through the central highlands, reaching the rugged northern deserts of Chihuahua and Sonora, where the *Norteños* have their own foods, like the incomparable *burrito*, beans, meat or eggs, and hot sauce rolled in a large flour tortilla. In dance halls he downed a few too many beers and danced the polka to lively northern *corrido* music, called *música norteña*. Backed with accordian, base and guitar, the *corrido* is a form of oral culture. Roving musicians would sing the news from town to town.

An important theme of contemporary Tex-Mex corridos is the plight of the undocumented immigrant, and René would listen to songs about himself, as he ordered another beer and danced with the barmaids.

René would eventually walk into the United States over an old railroad bridge and elude the immigration authorities. He had experienced a great deal of Mexico but without having visited any of the famous coastal resorts like Acapulco and Puerto Vallarta. He had missed the Mayan pyramids and had never seen the great city of Teotihuacán even though it lay only a hour away from his stone-cold, bare-walled hotel room in Mexico City. He had missed the tourist portion of Mexico, but knew his way around.

From his nightly get-togethers in raucous *cantinas,* René had learned all the regional stereotypes of Mexico. He could tell stories about the Yucatecos, the fiercely independent Mayans who are often the butt of ethnic jokes, perceived as slow-witted by other Mexicans who ignore the fact that the Yucatecos nearly gained their independence in the nineteenth century in a prolonged caste war.

Contemporary Mexico retains regional characteristics, sometimes from one town to the next. But the primary contradiction, the one that got René out of a jam, is the culture gap between lowlands and highlands. This phenomenon, called "the absurd divisiveness between highland and coast" by Francisco Maturana, coach of Ecuador's national football team, extends unevenly throughout the spine of Latin American, anywhere that high mountain regions give way to tropical lowlands.

In the lowlands, the tropical music is quick and syncopated, just as brisk as the pace of the Spanish language in Rene's El Salvador. In the highlands, the ranchera music moans with measured melancholy, a parallel to the more plodding but lucid Spanish of these cooler regions.

People in the hotlands (*tierra caliente*), perceive the highlanders as grim in spirit. People in *tierra fría* perceive the lowlanders as irresponsible and prone to violence and fits of passion.

Many states, including Puebla, Chiapas, Oaxaca, and Michoacán, contain both highlands and lowlands. In the invigorating pine forests of highland Michoacán, my inquiries helped locate a dirt road within hiking distance of the lowlands.

"But don't go down there," said the old machete-wielding peasant who had pointed out the road. "Down there, they're *matones* (killers)."

The vast differences in language, music, and pace of life between highland and lowland have precipitated stereotypes that contain an ounce of truth and a gallon of invention.

Human differences remain at the level of perception, but Mexico's physical differences are undeniable. If you like it hot and humid and don't mind mosquitos, choose the lush tropics. If you prefer eternal spring or brisk autumn weather and don't wish to do battle with those little flying pests, you may opt for a location in the highlands, where it will be easier, at first, to understand the local version of spoken Spanish.

A metropolitan setting to some extent mitigates the impact of regional differences. Both tropical Acapulco at sea level and highland Mexico City at 2,240 meters above sea level (7,347 ft) offer a more universal array of Mexican variables.

In general, the nearer you are to the center of the country, the more likely you will be in highland territory, while the nearer you are to the coastal extremities, the most probable that you'll experience lowland culture. Within the highlands, one may come across tight, deep valleys; one may walk from apple orchards to mango groves, shedding jacket, then sweater, then shirt, and then undershirt as the downward trek progresses.

Two rugged north-south mountain ranges, the Sierra Madre Occidental and the Sierra Madre Oriental cradle the high central plateau, which includes smaller mountain ranges and wide valleys well-suited for agriculture. More than half of Mexico's population lives in the central region, where serene lakes contain the rippling reflections of surrounding mountains. Chapala in Jalisco and Pátzcuaro in Michoacán are the largest of these lakes.

Much road travel in mountainous Mexico navegates over dramatic hairpin turns lined by crosses where fatal mistakes at the wheel have sent vehicle and occupants careening down a precipice, bouncing between cacti as in an old pinball machine.

Mexico's highest three mountains are found in the Cordillera Neovolcánica range, immediately to the south of Mexico City. On a rare pristine day in the city when the smog has washed away, observe Popcatépetl (5,452 meters) and Iztaccíhuatl (5,286 meters). The view from Puebla on the back side of these white- robed peaks is more likely unimpeded and quite stunning. Farther southeast in this same range, in the direction of Veracruz, is the majestic Pico de Orizaba (5,610 meters). Farther south, other mountain ranges crest within Oaxaca and Chiapas.

You don't have to be a pro to climb Popocatépetl, as friends of mine have proven. The easiest climb commences from the lodge at Tlacamas, at 3,950 meters, where with proper equipment, a climber in good physical shape and accustomed to high altitude and cold winds can make it up and down in a day.

CAUTION! Popocatepetl is a dormant but not extinct volcano. It started belching ash and sulphur dioxide for the first time in 70 years in 1994. Four climbers were caught over a sudden internal explosion and killed by "volcanic bullets" on April 30, 1996. El Popo's last major eruption was in the 9th century. As these pages are being written, El Popo is fuming again.

Consult the elderly *granizeros*, who communicate with the mountain's inner moods. Whether or not El Popo will soon be safe again to climb is a matter of controversy. Some consider the recent belching acts as an escape valve that relieves pressure and thus prevents a major eruption, while others believe an eruption is imminent. Check the Popo website on the internet before you climb!

For coastal enthusiasts, in general Mexico's more picturesque beaches are on the Pacific Ocean, with mountain ranges in sight. Beyond the Gulf of Mexico resorts, the more level beachlands of the Atlantic side attract fewer tourists. But with vast coastlands, solitary beachcombers will find their ideal spot on either side of Mexico. Both coasts receive the sweet waters of alternately serene and raging rivers flowing to the sea from the mountain gorges.

Why the difference between the highland and lowland cultures? No one knows for sure, but several theories exist. One theory goes back to the colonial period, tracing a greater influence of African cultures in the lowlands with a predominant influence of Native American cultures in the highlands. Whole populations of Indians transported by the Spaniards to work in the tropics were decimated by the hostile climate, with African slaves were brought in to fill the void.

Another theory suggests that Spaniards from the hotter regions of Spain such as Andalucía were more likely to colonize the tropics, with Spaniards from the cooler mountainous regions of their native country settling in Mexico's highlands. Spain has always been a regionalist country, and sharp local contrasts in Iberian speech patterns may have exerted an impact on regional Mexican Spanish.

Yet another theory ascribes a certain deterministic role to the climate. Mexico's coastal tropics and rainforests have been places of outdoor gathering and where one needs to speak more loudly to be heard (sounding more bombastic). In the cool highlands and colder cities like Toluca (at 2,680 meters), life would retreat between four walls, especially after sundown, and people could speak more intimately.

Whether or not any of these theories are valid, the major variable of physical setting as it effects way of life in Mexico is altitude. Indeed, during certain periods of Mexican history, Caribbean coastal areas such as Veracruz and Yucatán had closer ties with Cuba than with highland Mexico.

MEXICO FROM TOP TO BOTTOM WITH SELECTED FEATURES

With these mysteries of setting as an influence on character, we conclude this brief introduction to Mexico's physical setting with a handy list of the altitudes and other characteristics of major places of interest, many of which will be referred to in more detail in subsequent chapters. Listings will be in meters. To calculate feet above sea level, just multiply by 3.28. Population indicators: *multiple millions, **million plus, ***half million plus, ****100,000 plus, without any asterisk means smaller city.

Toluca*** Estado de México, 2,680. Friday Indian market (*tianguis*), attractive colonial center and museums, industrial parks.

Zacatecas** Zacatecas. 2,445. Mines financed superb colonial churches and buildings. View from Cerro de la Bufa. Off the main tourist path. Battle of Zacatecas, in which Villa defeated Huerta in 1914, is an example of brilliant military tactics.

Photo: Juan Carlos Vega

Although off the main tourist path, Zacatecas remains one of Mexico's most attractive colonial cities.

45

Tlaxcala, Tlaxcala, 2,252. for those who like colonial settings without throngs of tourists, just north of Puebla.

Mexico City* Federal District, 2,240 (known as *El D.F.*). Perhaps the most exciting city in the world but bring a machete to cut through the smog. Art, literature, music, murals, nightlife, indigenous ruins back-to-back with colonial masterpieces, distinct neighborhoods of character (La Zona Rosa, old downtown, colonial-bohemian Coyoacán), sinking cathedrals, Chapultepec forest, Maximilian's castle, the Museum of Anthropology, nearby pyramids of Teotihuacán to the north, crowded subways and buses, vast slums *(ciudades perdidas)*, and rising crime statistics. Author Elena Poniatowska describes Mexico City as "a black hole, a city on the edge of the abyss," while her colleague Carlos Monsiváis calls it "an unmanageable monster." Yet these and other writers and artists choose to remain right here!

Pátzcuaro, Michoacán, 2,175. Colonial-indigenous town, clean cobblestone streets, less than a 4-km walk to mellow Lake Pátzcuaro, surrounded by green mountains. Within the lake is the postcard fishing village, the isle of Janitzio, and north of Pátzcuaro are the P'urhépecha ruins of Tzintzuntzán. Wood products including furniture/artesanry.

Puebla** Puebla, 2,162. Colorful hand-painted mosaic tiles make its colonial architecture unique, numerous churches, conservative Catholicism, Nahua Indians, chicken in *mole* (an ancient sauce with two different hot peppers, sesame, nuts, sugar, and chocolate), Cinco de Mayo festival.

San Cristóbal de las Casas, Chiapas, 2,100. Closest city to Zapatista stronghold, Chamula culture, colorful colonial streets, pine forests, and the aroma of wood fires cooking at sunset.

Guanajuato**** Guanajuato, 2017. Most medieval-looking of Mexico cities, steep inclines reminding one of Italian hillside villages, mummies preserved by mineral content of soil, old mines, much culture and history. Muralist Rivera once banned from this city of his birth for his revolutionary ideas; today, there's a Rivera museum.

Photo: Juan Carlos Vega

Janitzio is an island fishing village surrounded by beautiful Lake Patzcuaro.

Morelia*** Michoacán, 1,910. University town, impressive stone aqueduct, Spanish colonial street scene, nearby lakes, especially Pátzcuaro. P'urhépecha(Tarascan) culture never conquered by Aztecs.

San Luis Potosí*** San Luis Potosí, 1,860. 16th century mining city with preserved colonial downtown and few tourists.

San Miguel Allende, 1,840. Most notable artists/writers' colony of Mexico, perfect climate in a colonial setting. Popularity has not yet led to its downfall, as North American settlers and Mexicans alike work to preserve the town's character, although gentrified town hardly resembles its bohemian yesterday. Mural painter Siqueiros once gave classes here, and Kerouac's *On The Road* hero Neal Cassady died here. Proximity to Guanajuato and continuing education courses are other pluses.

Aguascalientes*** Aguascalientes, 1,800. Thermal springs, clean, pleasant streets, and the most Mexican of all festivals, La Feria de San Marcos.

Taxco, Guerrero, 1,755, old silver mining town, perched breathtakingly on steep, green hillside, cobblestone streets, handmade silver jewelry. Are we in Disneyland-Mexico, or is this a real place?

Guadalajara* Jalisco, 1,563, second largest city, and capital of Mexican popular culture: tequila, mariachis, *charreadas* (rodeos), and traditional dances like the Mexican hat dance all come from Guadalajara. Lots of culture and pollution. Near beautiful Lake Chapala, a favorite Gringo retiree hideaway. Some of the best Orozco murals in public buildings.

Oaxaca**** Oaxaca (pronounced Wahaka), 1,550. Colonial architecture, unique black ceramic wares, Zapotec Indians, and the ancient ruins of the city in the sky, Monte Albán, looking down on Oaxaca. Home of Benito Juárez, with corresponding museum.

Cuernavaca*** Morelos, 1,542. Altitude is deceiving because the city is inclined, with its high part on the Mexico City side. Climate changes from one end to the other. Gardens, purple and rose bougainvilles clinging to walls, colonial architecture, traffic. First Mexican city to initiate prosperous Spanish language schools. Palacio de Cortés, nearby swimming-hole resorts. City has attracted writers, intellectuals like Ivan Illich.

Xalapa**** Veracruz, 1,427. Clean and green, temperate and colonial, university café life, and most important, a surreal mist that quite often occupies the city.

Chihuahua*** Chihuahua, 1,392. Museum of the Mexican Revolution, Pancho Villa territory, gateway to Chihuahua-Pacific Railroad that crosses the Barranca del Cobre (Copper Canyon): 20 canyons four times larger than the Grand Canyon: 39 bridges, 89 tunnels. Spectacular! Tip: one adventurer reports he got off at Creel and traveled with mailmen into canyons. Tarahumara cave-dweller territory. The 160 km "Tour de Tarahumara" is a foot-race through precarious canyon country in which the local Indians kick a small wooden ball. Tarahumarans invited to a Los Angeles marathon refused to participate when they discovered the race involved competition. It is legal for Tarahumaran sorcerers to consume hallucinogenic *peyote* when performing curative dances.

Ciudad Juarez*** 1,145. Borders El Paso, Texas, typical border-town business, dance halls, bars, inexpensive dentistry and auto repair, and prostitution, with American type suburbs far removed from the funky downtown. Smoke-stack manufacturing.

Monterrey* Nuevo León, 540. Third largest city, focal point for home-grown Mexican capitalism, U.S. style suburbs, modernist center, singular mountain backdrop of Cerro de la Silla (looks like sadddle on one-humped camel), hot and dry in summer, mild winters. Try the *cabrito* (baby goat).

Tuxtla-Gutiérrez**** Chiapas, 532. Colorful city with few tourists, and a bioregional zoo, plus nearby Sumidero Canyon. Breathtaking trip from tropical Tuxtla to highland San Cristóbal de las Casas.

Valladolid, Yucatán, sea level. Gateway to Mexico's most elaborate ruins Chichén Itzá, only 40 km away (see Strategic Directory), and an ideal spot to look down into the *cenotes*, expansive underground limestone water holes, a unique and impressive geographic phenomenon used by the Mayas and later the Spaniards as a source of water.

Acapulco** Guerrero, sea level. Pacific ocean resorts, daredevil divers at La Quebrada who fortunately hit the surf in the rocky crevasse below when the tide is high, water sports, discos, amusement parks. In spite of tourism, budget hotels still available near La Quebrada and downtown.

Manzanillo, Colima, sea level. Beaches, industry, port, lagoons. This might qualify as the funkiest of Mexico's Pacific Coast cities, an unbeatable double exposure of romantic beaches and industrial revolution soot. Only about 30 km from Barra de Navidad, a village reported to feature Mexico's best surfing waves.

Photo: Carlos Mendoza

Two cultures meet. Manzanillo doubles as a port and tourist resort.

Mazatlán*** Sinaloa, sea level. Beaches, fishing, and the towering El Faro lighthouse on a peak with a view of the city and coastline.

Mérida*** Yucatán, sea level. The capital of the Mayan culture, in a charming colonial setting, and gateway to Mayan ruins, including Chichén Itzá and Uxmal.

Puerto Vallarta**** sea level. Once secluded, now touristy, still maintains its rustic beauty, water sports, art galleries. One day people will forget that Tennessee Williams' *The Night of the Iguana*, 1964, was filmed here with Richard Burton, Elizabeth Taylor, Ava Gardner. Condominium timeshare capital of Mexico.

Tijuana*** sea level. One of the few, temperate, non-tropical coastal cities, thanks to the Japan Current. Built a Cultural Center to deflect its image of sin city, but sex and gambling are still big business. Raunchy dance halls, bars, and inexpensive lobster dinners on cliffs overlooking the sea. Auto repair and dentistry are thriving industries serving Americans who cross the border. Squatters in the hills and smoke-stack industry. Californians call it TJ.

Veracruz** Veracruz, sea level. Gulf of Mexico, party here with the *Jarochos* and their Huasteca music. Much more funky and raunchy than Acapulco. Big role in Mexican history, historic museums, especially the once-island prison fortress of San Juan de Ulúa. Try the *huachinango* (red snapper in spicy sauce).

Zihuatanejo, Guerrero, sea level. Less touristy than the nearby Ixtapa resort, the beach city of Zihuatanejo makes this list because it became the sanctuary for the two main characters from the gripping film *The Shawshank Redemption*.

Other sea-level beach resorts include Cancún, Isla Mujeres, and La Paz (Baja California).

Not included in this list are other cities, towns, rural regions, and mountain and coastal villages, attractive for their history, natural setting, or daily life. We shall visit some of these in later chapters.

– Chapter Three –

PROFILES

Mexico is a land of overstatement. One may use Cuernavaca's brilliant purple bougainville vines as a metaphor for Mexico's blatant sensuality. The green *nopal* plant, the prickly *tuna* fruit and the spiny *maguey* do for the northern deserts and central valleys of Mexico what dormers do for urban scenes in France, adding incomparable textures to otherwise commonplace scenes.

To call Puerto Vallarta a beach is like calling Beethoven's Ninth Symphony a song. Popocatépetl is not a mountain, it is a smoking mountain, and its snow-covered companion is a sleeping woman. The Copper Canyon is not one but twenty canyons.

Add the people to Mexico's physical setting and one finds more overstatement. Those bronze daredevils who dive from Acapulco's La Quebrada bluff into the rocky Pacific splash a great message: that Mexico's physical setting is an invitation to be seen or heard, to paint in warm brilliant colors like Tamayo, to build monuments that will last for eternity, like Teotihuacán or Palenque, to adorn the walls of public buildings with brilliant murals, to create an ugly ocher soup over Mexico City that makes Los Angeles smog seem like an innocuous mist.

The *picante* in Mexican food mirrors the piquant of Mexico's character. Justice, in Chihuahua's "Monument to Justice" is sensual expression, revolutionary nudity.

"Sum up in a word what makes Mexican people different from those of countries with a similar heritage," I asked a Mexican friend who had traveled and lived abroad.

"Chispa" he said, which translates roughly into "spark." In the following pages we shall meet some of the characters who set off the spark of Mexican life.

PANCHO VILLA AND THE MAN WHO SAVED HIM

The first great social uprising of the 20th century, the Mexican Revolution, was fought between 1910 and 1920. By the time I had an opportunity to interview participants in that cataclysmic saga, I was a student in the 1970s and most of the veterans of the revolution were dead.

By word of mouth, I traced an irregular route to the doors of three men who participated in the attack on Columbus, New Mexico in 1916, one of whom, Lauro Trevizo, still had a bullet lodged under his arm. To find Mr. Trevizo, I had to drive through rutty old exhaust-pipe scraping ranch roads to the town of Namiquipa, in Chihuahua. Trevizo asserted with vehemence that Villa had attacked Columbus after having been tricked by the arms salesman of that town, and embargoed by President Wilson.

I would also locate a former *soldadera,* María Cortés Espinoza, reputedly over a hundred years old. "What did it feel like to kill for the first time?" I asked.

"I didn't feel anything," María said. "And don't think that I've mellowed now that I'm an old hag."

53

Arnulfo Hernánez Arcos told me how the villagers of Morelos supported his Zapatistas: "The women of Jolalpan and Asuchapan cultivated marijuana, went to the *Federales*, and exchanged it for arms."

According to legend, the Villistas punished villages like Namiquipa for having supported Villista rivals. Long before contemporary psychologists discovered that rape was an act of violence, the villistas raped the women of Namiquipa as a message to all those other villages that would dare contemplate switching to the side of Carranza.

"Is this legend true?" I asked a few women in Namiquipa. "Yes, it's true," responded an elderly woman in a patterned *rebozo* (grey shawl). "But it didn't happen to me."

More than proving or disproving legends, I was intrigued by personalities. Here is a collage of quotes from people whose paths crossed with Pancho Villa, from different villages of Villa's northern Mexican stronghold:

"I was a child when Villa arrived at my house one day and said: *Let's see, kid, catch that chicken for me and I'll give you this coin.*"

"Villa arrived at my town when I was playing *frontón* [a game similar to squash]. The man played with us. He was clumsy because he didn't take off his bullet belt or holster."

"I saw Villa kill two of his soldiers who were trying to break in and loot a house."

"General Villa began to kill people (in Zacatecas) to stop the looting of the city."

"Villa arrived and called a meeting of the whole town. He had my father say which ones were not burdened with obligations to support a family. He took with him 23 youngsters between 18 and 21."

Devoted Villista Lauro Trevizo admits: "During the final hours of the Revolution, after so many betrayals, Pancho Villa became cruel. Everything went wrong: the defective weapons and arms they sold him in Columbus, the generals who turned their backs on him, and Carranza and Obregon's *defensas sociales* (villages organized to oppose the Villistas).

"After that, for Villa, it was kill, kill, kill, and cut off their ears."

I then asked Trevizo to comment on modern Mexico. "Today in Mexico," he said, "we need another Pancho Villa."

Many of the veterans lived in deplorable conditions sixty years after they'd fought. A one hundred-year-old Yaqui Indian was still working, selling lottery tickets in Torreón. The Yaquis had been the first to oppose the Porfirio Díaz dictatorship, while subjected to forced cross-country marches from north to south. Those who survived were forced into slave labor.

"We fought Porfirio Díaz with stones and arrows," he said, his voice breaking in emotion with the words "all of us, men, women and children."

"So that they would fight harder," said Arnulfo Hernández Arcos, "Obregón told the Yaquis: *If today you're killed, tomorrow you'll wake up with your families.*"

After the 1916 Villa attack on Columbus, New Mexico, the United States sent what was called "The Punitive Expedition" into northern Mexico. Histories on both sides of the border explain that General Pershing failed to capture Pancho Villa when the villagers in Chihuahua refused to give Pershing's men a shred of information about Villa.

"Nonsense," said Villista General Nicolás Fernández, who at the age of 95, had a grim office in Torreón.

From his empty desk in a room with bare walls and only one hard wooden chair for a visitor, Fernández set the ground rules of our interview. I was not to ask him any questions because the slightest distraction impaired his recollections. Speaking for three hours straight, interrupted only by sips of water, the tall and gritty old man narrated his history of the revolution in a raspy voice.

Fernández sidestepped references to ideology, but for oft-heard phrases like "we told our men that we wanted to rid the yoke from our neck." The word for "neck" was *pescuezo* which refers to the neck of an animal, the implication that pre-Revolution Mexicans were nothing more than beasts of burden.

Fernández called me naive to believe that, after beatings and the threat of torture, there wouldn't be at least one or two Chihuahuans in each village who would bend to the pressure of the Pershing forces and betray Pancho Villa.

For this reason, Fernández and his men traveled from village to village with a covered wagon. Inside the wagon, they told village onlookers, was a wounded Pancho Villa too ill to come out and give his greetings.

The wagon, however, was an empty decoy, traveling deeper and deeper into the dense mountains, away from the cavernous hideaway of Pancho Villa. The decoy was working, as here and there, villagers would tell Pershing's men something to the effect that "he went that way," pointing of course in the direction of the empty covered wagon.

Fernández's retreating soldiers would later have a skirmish or two with Pershing's men. Once far removed from the Villa hideout, the men of Nicolás Fernández disappeared into the virtually impenetrable Sierra Madre Occidental.

Ironically, prior to the President Wilson arms embargo against Villa, Generals Villa and Pershing were to pose side by side with beaming smiles in a now-famous photograph.

Today, the roads taken by the Pershing Expedition are in better condition, although few are paved. Visitors wishing to trace the event may obtain maps from the Chamber of Commerce in Columbus, New Mexico, a town that is now proud to have been torched by the men of Pancho Villa. (Phone: 505-531-2708)

The mountains of Chihuahua are quite rugged and primitive. Be prepared for a rough trek.

With such a lengthy interview, I felt I had overly imposed on Fernández. But the stern general flashed his first smile at the end of the session.

"I'm not as strong as I used to be. I think I've told you the whole story. Now I must take a nap."

Nicolás Fernández, fourth from left, Pancho Villa's right-hand man, here in the company of some pretty tough soldaderas, women who fought valiantly in the Mexican Revolution.

(In Chihuahua, visit the Museo Histórico de la Revolución, Quinta Luz. Pancho Villa had several wives. After he was murdered in 1923, Luz Corral won a verdict declaring her Villa's legal wife. The Chihuahua mansion she won in the verdict was transformed into a museum in 1981. Among the Villa memorabilia is the bullet-riddled Dodge he was driving when shot down. Calle 10a, just past Mendez.)

CHAMULA INDIANS: SAN CRISTÓBAL DE LAS CASAS

The vast expanse of Mexico's northern deserts was the ideal location for Pancho Villa's horsemen to rebel against the feudal landlords more than eight decades ago. Southern Chiapas, the antithesis of arid Chihuahua with its cool pine forest mountains and steamy jungles, is the setting for a new version of revolution, at once more modern, reaching out to the international human rights community, and more ancient, deriving energy from Mayan traditions.

San Cristóbal de las Casas, in the heart of the highlands of Chiapas, was named after the Dominican Friar Bartolomé de las Casas, the "Defender of the Indians." More than 450 years after Friar de las Casas raised his voice for Indian's rights, the Mayan ancestors in Chiapas, the Tzotzils and the Tzeltals, remain among the most oppressed of Mexico's numerous indigenous communities.

Among the Tzotzils, the Chamulas, centered in nearby San Juan Chamula, were the most rebellious. In 1524, they fiercely resisted the Spaniard invaders. In 1869, with mestizos now in the visible positions of power, the Chamulas launched a rebellion against mestizo domination. A few initial victories proved illusory and the rebellion was squelched.

I arrived late one afternoon in San Cristóbal with the intention of getting to know the Chamulas. It was market day and I went straight to the market district. I knew in advance that the Chamulas were a tightknit clan historically suspicious of outsiders. The best way to scare off potentially hospitable people from this region is to tote a camera, so I left mine under the seat of my old Chevy.

San Cristóbal is reached by a spectacular winding road from tropical Tuxtla-Gutiérrez 1,600 meters below in less than two hours. As the highway threads its way upward, banana trees cede to pine forests.

The fatiguing humidity below was replaced by a cool nip in the July air, perfumed with the aroma of *ocote* wood fires as most of San Cristóbal prepared for dinner. The pastel colors of the colonial facades added a touch of warmth as the sun vanished behind the forested hills.

I ate at a market stall and began talking with the Chamulas, mainly asking for information. The winning question turned out to be "Where can I find a cheap hotel?"

As darkness set in, one of a group of conversing Chamulas, dressed in a white wool tunic and sandals, said he was on his way to their hotel should I wish to accompany him.

Once inside the old hotel, I paid the woman attendant a few pesos and was given a *petate* and a space on the floor of a large, collective bedroom.

The real "nightlife" in San Cristóbal involves the art of conversation. My "guide" narrated the plight of the Chamulas. Others on nearby *petates* joined in.

Some young men from their community had sought out fortune in Mexico City. Their typical sagas ended in tragic failure: unskilled labor at below-subsistence wages, violent attacks in overcrowded *vecindades* (tenement slums) where swarms of roomers shared a single malfunctioning bathroom, loneliness in the absence of community leading to alcoholism. A naive Chamula in Mexico City was easy prey for scam artists and unscrupulous employers. The best endings of these prototypical plots saw the Chamula brother returning to his community.

The first person singular did not exist in the discourse of my companion, whose story was narrated entirely in the *nosotros* (we):

"We once had the illusion that we could send our people to the city and they could help us out," said my self-appointed guide in broken Spanish. "But in the city, they learn to become selfish. If they make a little money, they forget who paid their bus fare.

"No matter how bad it gets here, we no longer encourage our people to leave the community."

I'm not sure that I learned much more than I would have from reading books like Ricardo Pozas' *Juan Pérez Jolote: Biografía de un Tzotzil*. However spending the night as part of a community and observing a collective existence totally foreign to my own individualistic background represented an intangible type of learning experience.

Indigenous intellectuals, both Indian and non-Indian, have been arriving at the same conclusions as my Chamula companion. Dr. José

Photo: Roberto Gaudelli

An Indigenous woman finds subsistence against the odds.

María Muriá, historian and director of the prestigious Colegio de Jalisco, explains how the approach to values of the individual has been exemplary in Mexican schools. "However, when it comes to our collective beings, the attitude has been completely different. The example to follow," he criticizes, "will always be foreign, an imported formula to resolve our problems, a formula which is alien to our model of civilization."

Over the years there has been little relief from the harshness of Chamula life but for the mellowness that comes from within their collective support system. Their Catholicism, rooted in their pre-colonial religion, has been manipulated by local mestizo *caciques* for economic gain. According to a disquieting Radio France International report, the PRI-hired caciques have three main businesses connected to Chamula Catholic rituals: soft drinks like Coca Cola, used in purification ceremonies, candles, prominent in virtually every religious event, and liquor (*aguardiente*), consumed in festivals and ceremonies "to show gratefulness to the gods."

As the Zapatistas oppose the caciques and their PRI benefactors, many Chamulas bypass the insurgency and seek a less demanding solution, joining evangelist sects which oppose soft drinks, shun symbolic adornments like candles, and prohibit drinking. Chamula women married to heavy drinkers are especially attracted to the evangelist churches.

But a clearly-defined good guy-bad guy scenario is hard to discern. The evangelist churches may liberate their newcomers from expensive religious rituals, but they preach a type of individualism that nullifies the collective Chamula support network. Meanwhile, in the tradition of Bartolomé de las Casas, a coterie of Catholic priests raise their voices in defense of the Indians, led by Bishop Samuel Ruiz García. Ruiz García is labeled *El Obispo Rojo* (The Red Bishop) by indignant landowners and políticos.

Radio France International estimates that many of the 30,000 Chamulas in San Cristóbal are *expulsados* from their communities and become Zapatista sympathizers. Violent incidents are reported between Catholics and evangelists, fomented by caciques faced with the prospect of losing their three cash cows, soft drinks, candles and liquor.

One Chamula child relates that he hid under his bed to escape the bullets of attackers outside his house. He believes the assault was brought on by his family's evangelism.

According to Father Michel, a French priest who has worked in Chiapas for more than 30 years, the main conflict used to be between Indians and mestizos, but today it is between Indians and Indians. In his village of 35,000, there are 14,000 traditional Catholics, 6,000 Protestants of five different sects, and 10,000 followers of the Catholic "theology of liberation." He reported in mid-1997 that aid programs from the government are intended to diminish support for the Zapatistas but that "sympathizers of the Zapatistas are becoming increasingly numerous."

Such confusion from within the Indian communities does not prevent progressives in Chiapas from lending creative support for the movement to undo semi-feudal structures and enfranchise the Indians. A theatre group, for example, travels from school to school presenting a marionette show on children's rights. One of the rights contradicts the orthodox free market policies of the central government; the marionettes affirm that when parents are not able to provide the basic necessities to their children, the government has an obligation to step in and do so.

One child interviewed by Radio France International mentioned that his father takes him down to *tierra caliente* to work on the coffee plantations. Traditionally on these plantations, Chamulas would be lent an amount of money up front by the coffee grower and then would find it difficult to pay back the loan, with the high price of basic necessities at stores owned by the grower himself. This *sistema de enganche* was just one more way in which the Chamulas encountered obstacles wherever they went.

The spirit of community, the Chamula's basic survival mechanism, may dissipate with the evangelist sects.

As these conflicts evolve, the highlands of Chiapas retain their inherent charm. As in nearby Guatemala, each highland village has its distinct dress. Weavers' cooperatives organized by local Tzotzil and Tzeltal women help preserve and revive folk art, using traditional dyes from plants and trees.

Visitors considering getting to know Indian villages surrounding San Cristóbal should play it safe and go in the company of a moderately-priced day tours. Tour agencies are conveniently located within walking distance of El Zócalo. Should you wish to go into business in the area, for your own peace of mind, choose a product other than soft drinks, candles, and liquor.

To soak in the local culture, first ask for information at the Tourist Office (Zócalo/Palacio Municipal). Visit the Chamula women's craft market (Templo de Santo Domingo and La Caridad), the Museo de

Arqueólogía, Etnografía, Historia y Arte (next to Santo Domingo), the Centro Cultural El Puente, the market, and Na Bolom (the house of now-deceased Swiss anthropologists).

Will the Zapatistas find "political" operating space within the current democratic opening, or will Mexico's first free elections in nearly seven decades fail to make a dent in the semi-feudal economy of Chiapas? Will the the government continue a "low intensity" war against the Zapatistas? If so, will the Zapatistas choose to escalate their insurgency. Those who wish to visit this region would do well to keep abreast of the latest developments.

THE MECHANICS OF SURVIVAL

In Chiapas, desperate living conditions have sown the seeds of rebellion. But most of Mexico's downtrodden survive through less drastic measures, some involving creative mechanics.

If it's broken, they say, Mexicans can fix it. With this in mind, I bought an old "three-door" Chevy for the price of scrap iron. The engine ran smooth enough but the right front door had been irreparably smashed in. At U.S. body shops they warned me that the mangled frame made it absolutely impossible to install a new door.

I drove it to Mexico. In Tlalnepantla, an industrial city to the north of Mexico City, I found Mario. Actually, it was Mario who found me. He walked up to the Chevy wielding a hammer.

"Would you like me to fix it?"

Mario was a freelance mechanic. He owned neither workshop nor fancy tools. He would borrow the tools from a friend. The job would be done on the street of the slum where he lived. In a middle class, residential neighborhood, there would be no toleration for the incessant hammering noises coming from my sculptor-mechanic. But here, the street was available for an array of repairs, from simple oil changes to ring jobs. Long before the throwaway culture had been first questioned by ecologists, recycling and resuscitation of dead objects was the way of life in this type of neighborhood.

After Mario's first day of labor, I wondered whether I had committed a grave error in advancing a down payment. His neighbors warned me that he was a pathological liar. Their assertions were confirmed when he told me with a broad smile on his cheerfully round face that his grandmother was "the Countess of Guanajuato."

The hammering continued, drowning out the ranchera singers who bellowed from a music store on the corner.

In less than two weeks, the job was done. My only regret is not having taken before-and-after pictures.

Weeks later, I watched Manuel take apart my carburettor piece by piece, find the failing part, clean each piece meticulously, and put it back together.

"I worked in California," Manuel said. "But over there, they're not mechanics. They're part changers."

On a ranch in Michoacán, I listened to rancher José's truck shaking and quaking. "We're missing a part," José said, as he opened the hood and inserted a piece of carefully folded paper.

"That'll solve the problem temporarily until I can drive to town and get the part."

In Mexico, those people who lack other means depend on the mechanics of survival. I watched one gentleman in a rural area of the State of Mexico start up the electricity in his makeshift adobe house by connecting a wire to the electric company's lines. He called it "stealing electricity."

Back in Tlalnepantla, I had an old TV that was hopelessly condemned.

"What'll I do with this thing," I asked Mario.

"Just leave it out in the street. Someone who needs it will pick it up and fix it."

I left it on a street in front of an empty lot at 2:00 pm. When I passed by three hours later, the TV was gone. No doubt it was already showing the evening soap opera in someone's shack.

TRUCK DRIVERS AND THE ROAD TO LINARES

A most bizarre story of making the unworkable work began one night outside a gas station on Highway 57 in San Luis Potosí. Mariano and Guillermo came out of the gas station restaurant, saw me with my thumb out, and offered me a ride.

"Our truck goes 25 kilometers per hour, max," Mariano said. "But we hook up with a friend's truck and he pulls us along."

It was dark and I feared being left without a ride. This was the first time I'd hitchhiked in Mexico, and I didn't know at the time that it pays to only accept the most comfortable and dependable rides.

I sat in the middle of the cabin, between Mariano and Guillermo. Their truck was roped with a thick cord to the back bumper of their friend's vehicle. We must have been traveling about 80 kph. But somewhere near Huizache, they halted and separated the two vehicles.

Mariano explained that a police checkpoint lay just ahead. Their friend would be waiting for them beyond the checkpoint and we'd hook up again. We crawled by the checkpoint at 20 kph and later hooked up.

TR/86

Deep into the night darkness, with the Milky Way lighting up the desert, we halted at the juncture where Route 57 continues north and Route 60 crosses the Sierra Madre Oriental. Mariano explained that "we've lost our locomotive." The fast truck would continue due north on 57. Mariano would cross over to Linares on 60.

On the map, it was a short red line to Linares. I decided to stay aboard.

What I didn't know was that the first half of this stretch was all uphill, until the connector road to Galeana. We advanced so slowly that a Tarahumara uphill runner would have left us in his wake. The lights of passing trucks created the illusion that we were backing down, not creeping up.

"Don't worry," Mariano consoled me. "We'll make up for the lost time on the way down."

Some time past midnight, we stopped at an old adobe house that turned out to be a restaurant. They served us *frijoles de olla* (bean soup cooked in a ceramic pot) with tortillas and hot chile peppers. Among the hot peppers was the tiny atomic-powered *chile piquín,* which Mariano insisted that I try if I ever wanted to be a good Mexican. This warm food at the edge of the frosty pine forest was one of the most memorable and tasty meals I've ever enjoyed.

As we moved on through the night, Mariano and Guillermo took turns dozing off. For me the *chile piquín* had proven more effective than NODOZE or espresso. I would later summon the best meditating techniques I knew in order to catch a few minutes (or were they hours?) of sleep. Somewhere deep in the wooded mountains, in the caves and canyons around Iturbide, were the old campfire sites of the greedy characters in B. Traven's *The Treasure of Sierra Madre.*

I was rudely awaken by a sharp turn that sent me crunching into the stocky Guillermo at my right. The sun was rising and we were beginning our descent.

Now I understood what Mariano meant by making up for the lost time. The truck was careening around hairpin turns, past the makeshift graves and crosses of those who had died after losing control of their vehicles, past a massive bas-relief sculpture cut out of a mountain wall, dedicated by sculptor Francisco Cantú to the heroes who built this road. The more treacherous the turns, the more sparkling the glee beneath the bushy eyebrows of Mariano. For Mariano, this road was a virtual reality video game, where a losing manoeuvre would lead to certain death.

Tour guides called this a scenic road, but for me it was a nightmare that began at dawn.

"Don't worry, my friend," Guillermo said. "Mariano knows this road better than anyone. We will get you to Linares safe and sound."

On blind turns, Mariano would sometimes honk his horn to warn possible approaching motorists. But most of the time, he deduced from the snaking road directly below us that nothing was coming up.

"Only a mountain lion leaping across the road can stop us now," Mariano laughed. As the road began to level off, through our windows was a double exposure of desert and tropical vegetation.

Linares, their destiny, is a bustling citrus-growing city with few or no tourists, and no significant attraction. To me it was the greatest place I'd ever seen in Mexico.

I bid farewell to my cheerful companions. A few years later, in my old Chevy, near Tula, Hidalgo, I would spin off the road into a ditch to avoid a herd of burros, and I would remember, too late, Mariano's assertion that "the straight roads are more dangerous because drivers take fewer precautions." My car was pulled out by a truck driver.

On another occasion, in the zero visibility of a Gulf of Mexico torrential rain, I swerved off the road into what looked like an irrigation ditch, south of Matamoros.

No truck driver will stop for me now, I thought, not in the pouring rain.

Yet, within minutes, a truck pulled off the road. The driver descended from his cabin with a ball of cord. After he tugged the Chevy out of the rut, we chatted over a bottle of Carta Blanca in a bamboo-walled restaurant a mile up the road.

Mexican truck drivers often get a bad rap. With tough times after multiple devaluations, they seem less likely today to stop for a vehicle in distress. But I still consider them as the Guardians of the Road.

Besides, it seems that every time you see the *Angeles Verdes* (Green Angels), English/Spanish mechanics in green rescue trucks, your car is running just fine. If you are lucky enough to see them pass by just when you break down, they'll provide minor service for free, including parts, labor, and fuel. Or, if you plan it right and break down near a phone, call 5-250-01-23-51.

Those who decide to take the definite risk of hitchhiking, carry a sign (mine said GRINGO AL NORTE on one side and GRINGO AL SUR on the other). Dress clean-cut. If the final destiny of your benefactor is in the middle of nowhere, ask to get out earlier, at a gas station or at the edge of a town. I've hitched to many places in Mexico and learned that as entertaining as truck drivers like Mariano and Guillermo are, it's best to wait for a private automobile.

Remember that you are taking a risk when you hitchhike.

POLICE

Hitching may be safer than driving. It's not rare to hear of truck and bus drivers fleeing after an accident, leaving their vehicles behind forever. In Mexican law, drivers involved in an accident are assumed to be guilty until proven innocent. Go prove it was not your fault if your only witness is dead.

"Nowadays," one Mexico City resident told me, "if you've been victimized by a burglary or accident and you see the police coming, instead of welcoming them, you flee."

During the first three months of 1994, 229 law-enforcement agents were incarcerated for crimes such as car thefts, burglaries, assaults, murders, narcotics trafficking, and even protecting drug lords, according to a September 27, 1996 article in *Commonweal*.

Truck drivers, too, have often complained to me about police shakedowns.

Years ago, a District Attorney in Mexico City got rid of the whole police department and hired idealistic students instead. After a few years, corruption as usual had returned. Mexicans often refer to police as *mordelones* (big biters) because they seek *mordidas* (bribes, literally "bites"). In June of 1996, President Ernesto Zedillo replaced Mexico City's seventeen top law-enforcement officials with army generals and colonels.

One survey revealed that Mexico City residents have "little" (34 percent) or "no" (52 percent) confidence in their municipal police.

Some Mexicans look at the bribery scenario more positively. Why not pay the fine on the spot, they say, rather than waste a day in court? The system eliminates the middleman. Underpaid policeman (they earn about $200 per month) are expected to take care of things out in the field – expected to do so by their superiors, as compensation for the low salaries.

Knowing this, I once took a chance after getting side-swiped in the middle of a busy Mexico City *glorieta* (traffic circle). The man who hit me had a long chat with Officer Friendly, after which he (the driver) asked me to "resolve it here," expecting that I'd pay him. My cynical Mexican passengers insisted that my antagonist had already paid off the cop in advance.

"Vamos a la delegación" (let's go to the precinct), I said. I figured that I had a better chance in the precinct since a cop bringing his traffic problems to his superiors is like a city boy taking his street conflicts to mama. We followed the patrol car to the precinct. As the two drivers, my antagonist and I, waited in the dingy corridor, our (his) policeman disappeared. Why not? The man had already collected.

When my antagonist discovered that his ally had disappeared into the polluted mist of Mexico City, he suddenly turned friendly, if you consider trembling a sign of friendliness. "What do you say we forget the whole thing?" he suggested. At that point, I probably could have gotten a few bucks from him, but with only a minor scrape, I was content with the moral victory. The precinct cops behind the desks didn't want us to stick around anyway, so we left.

The city of Chihuahua hired international consultants to help root out police corruption. Police were removed from patrol cars and put on bicycles, where they could interact with the citizenry.

Without condoning police corruption, there's a lot to be said about a system that resolves problems right on the spot: fewer judges, fewer lawyers, shorter court calendars, less tax money going to police salaries, with their income derived directly from those who "receive the service."

So I'm not going to knock the Mexican police. They're too easy a target. And besides, in those cities like Chihuahua, where the cops are out on bicycles in a much more intimate relationship with the citizenry, their presence is welcomed. Chihuahua governor Patricio Martínez hired U.S. consultants to train his municipal police and it seems to have paid off.

JOURNALISTS

When the government really wants to crack down, it has employed private goons rather than police. The victims were often journalists, and more than a few muckrakers have been executed gangland style. In most cases, however, it was neater and cleaner to simply "guide" the media.

For many years, the magazine *Proceso* was the only truly critical journal, more easily tolerated by ruling cliques. It's intellectual language and higher cost make it less accessible to a general public.

Meanwhile, the internationally-recognized caricaturist Rius found a way to reach the masses, producing comic books such as *Los Supermachos* and *Los Agachados*. Rius confronted Mexican themes of political culture and machismo, but also wrote a series of books with more universal themes that were widely translated and distributed abroad. The exquisite but critical humor of Rius and the vast following it generated allowed him to take liberties that most "straight" commentators would not get away with.

Mexico seemed to me like a bastion of freedom of expression, on one occasion, when the militarized border guards in El Salvador confiscated a Rius comic of mine, labeling it "subversive."

In the realm of TV, for decades Emilio Azcárraga's Televisa company of four TV networks and 16 radio stations unabashedly supported the status quo. Azcárraga once called himself a "soldier of the president," and responded to criticism by affirming that a television company's responsibility was "to entertain the poor and distract them from their sad reality and difficult future."

As embarrassed ex-President Carlos Salinas de Gortari finds refuge in self-imposed exile, he can be credited with having opened the doors to a freer press. "In accordance with his economic liberalization program," wrote the *Columbia Journalism Review*, "Salinas allowed the importation of newsprint ... and sold off a government-owned television station," with the new TV Azteca finally triggering media competition.

In 1997, Televisa's Emilio Azcárraga died of cancer at the age of 66. Televisa remains the property of his family, but there have been signs (interviews with opposition candidates, for example) that its programming will become less demagogic.

Even in this context of new freedoms for journalists, old guard políticos still exercised power. Independent journalist Razhy González was kidnapped late in 1996 by government agents as he was leaving his office in Oaxaca. He was roughed up and interrogated for 45 hours by men who accused him of being a spy for a Oaxaca guerrilla group. (González had a knack for landing interviews with guerrilla leaders in Chiapas, Oaxaca and Guerrero.)

Commenting on the kidnapping, Oaxaca governor Diodoro Carrasco Altamirano's words were ominous.

"Now is not the moment to play around with critical journalism," he said, shortly after González was released.

Several independent newspapers have been increasing in circulation as the public responds positively to aggressive news coverage. But paid government press releases poorly disguised as news articles are still printed, identified as *gacetillas*.

A 1997 pre-election report by the French journalist group Reporters Sans Frontiers named Mexico as one of the countries where murderers and harassers of journalists remain unpunished. With the opposition victory in the July 1997 elections, journalists emerged victorious in their decades-long tug-of-war with officialdom.

Pioneer heroes in independent news coverage were publications like *Zeta* (Tijuana), *Siglo 21* (Guadalajara), *El Imparcial* (Hermosillo), Gonzalez's *Contrapunto* (Oaxaca), *La Jornada* (Mexico City), and the national weekly *Proceso*.

LA CASA CHICA AND THE SEX INDUSTRY

The great novelist and essayist Carlos Fuentes is a leading voice in a worthy tradition of culturally self-critical Mexican literature.

In Fuentes' first novel, *Where the Air is Clear*, he unmasks one of Mexico's fabled cultural institutions, *La Casa Chica* (the little household). Married men of all social classes commonly keep mistresses in well-equipped apartments *(casas chicas)*.

But Mexico's recent economic crises have put a damper on this extravagant custom and at least one macho, after having become bankrupt in his fatal attempt to maintain two households, committed suicide.

"According to some estimates, tens of thousands of single women rely on the casa chica tradition for much of their livelihood," writes Tim Padgett in *Newsweek*.

As it becomes increasingly difficult to maintain a casa chica, some mistresses have formed support groups, called *Las Número Dos* (The Numbers Twos), a "natural sorority," according to one of the mistresses.

Strip Joints

In a 1996 *Guardian* article, Phil Gunson surmises that as the economy slumps, the sex industry rises, and strip clubs with optional prostitution flourish. Pedro Peñalosa, who chaired the public safety committee of Mexico City's legislative assembly, said that "in one capital district – Cuauhtemoc – 1,217 clubs of this kind were operating."

One stripper from a better club said she earned US$2,250 a month, twice what she took home as a saleswoman selling reconditioned motors.

"The problem is" she is quoted by Gunson, "that if you have a good body, most bosses want to get you in the sack." Ironically, she feels safer taking her clothes off in public.

But remarkably uninhibited strip joints in the mold of the legendary Teatro Iris have existed for a long time, one indication of the moral flexibility the Latin American brand of Catholicism.

Cross the border and loosen up. Most commentary about the long border between Mexico and the United States refers to the economic gap between the two countries. "Geographically Mexico is the only third world country that borders with a developed country," explains one Mexican diplomat. But the culture gap may be even more significant than the obvious economic disparities. Every weekend, thousands of Texans and Arizonans from Bible Belt regions cross over the Mexican border in order to shed the inhibitions imposed by evangelical fundamentalism.

Strip joints on the U.S. side of the border are generally corporate and impersonal. In a Mexican strip joint, if you're seated in the first row and do not jump up from your seat and attempt to kiss the stripper, the crowd will taunt you as a coward.

Prostitutes

In a raunchy border city bar, I invited one prostitute to a drink, letting her know in advance that I was there only to do an interview.

She whispered, "don't bother with mixed drinks. They'll charge you for the rum and coke and I'll get only the coke. Just order a soda."

It was a slow night anyway, she explained, and she preferred to relax. Her professional name was *Muñeca* (Doll).

Muñeca reserved her true love for her boyfriend, she explained. The rest was strictly business, and she felt "absolutely no erotic pleasure in the practice of the trade". She considered herself an entertainer, and added that the only reason she was in the business was economics.

The Mexican sex industry can get quite theatrical compared to parallel industries in more somber countries. But, as my interviewee reiterated, it all boiled down to the fact that rampant poverty left no alternative for many women.

Her assertion is backed up by a 1997 report in the California weekly *La Voz Latina* on the City of San Luis Potosí. The report asserts that the neoliberal economic policies of the past two six-year-term presidencies have exacerbated the gap between rich and poor, leaving prostitution as an only alternative for an increasing number of women. An estimated one thousand prostitutes are now found in San Luis Potosí alone, half of those with *padrotes* (pimps). Three hundred hang out in the "historic center" of the city.

The State Commission on Human Rights denounced the city police for harassment and repression against the sexual workers. Many of the women were under 20 years of age and had been brought into the city from other parts of Mexico. In most Mexican cities, prostitution is legal within a *zona de tolerancia* and the women must report to health clinics for weekly examinations. Such exams won't help if the previous unprotected trick carried a venereal disease or AIDS.

MACHOS

For years, irresponsible magazine articles have reinforced the cliche that *machismo* (male chauvinism) somehow originated in Mexico. By making such assertions, these pseudo-sociologists insult Arabs, Spaniards, Orthodox Jews, Mormons in Utah, Japanese, Rambo, the Mattel Toy Corporation, and so many other persons, peoples, or entities who in one way or another pass down from one generation to another customs of male dominance. Before any discussion of the Mexican version of machismo, it must be stipulated that virtually every culture in the world, save certain matriarchal societies, have nurtured their own versions of machismo. Within Mexico, in Tehuantepec and in an isolated region of Michoacán, one may find matriarchal communities.

The particular brand of Mexican machismo must be traced back to the Spanish Golden Age, the 1600s. A major theme of Golden Age literature is appearance versus reality. Mothers, wives, and daughters must maintain a public appearance of faithfulness or purity. The honor of their sons, husbands and fathers depends on this faithfulness or chastity. What happens behind closed doors is hardly relevant as long as it remains secretive. But what the public perceives in the behavior of these women, whether the perception is objective or not, determines the vital honor of the male in this other-directed society.

Don Juan Tenorio, for example, did not "conquer" women so much for sexual pleasure as to prove his manhood to the rest of the world. Theses have been written suggesting that Don Juan's sexual conquests were needed to assuage self-doubts regarding his manhood.

An insult to mother, wife, daughter means that son, husband, father must avenge the woman-symbol in a duel with the individual who taunted her.

If a faithful wife is believed to be unfaithful by the community, then she must be killed by her husband to cleanse his honor. (Remember we're in 17th century Spain.) Reality or truth are relatively meaningless in regards to a man's self-image, but public perception is crucial. Similar values are held in relation to the chastity of the man's daughter. In order to protect the reputation of her father, she must maintain appearances of virginity.

Mexican *charro* (cowboy) movies resemble the dramas of the Spanish Golden Age 300 years earlier. An affront to the woman in a man's life, if witnessed by others or known to the community, must be avenged in blood.

The charro exhibits machismo not only in his sexual dominance but in exhibitions of bravery in *charreadas* (Mexican rodeos). Bull fighting, inherited from Spain, is another avenue for males to exhibit their valor, although this ritual is only popular among a reduced sector of fanatic devotees.

Macho women. In the extended aftermath of the 1910 revolution, the concept of honor in Mexican charro movies would be forever transformed from the Golden Age model. The daring bravery of *soldadera* horsewomen during the revolution would engender tough women characters typified by actress María Félix. Cultural historians may wish to find the missing link between the macha-women characters in Mexican cinema and the sexually-dominant *serrana* characters in Medieval Spanish literature. Coincidentally, a modern-day *serrana* in Mexican music and cinema is named Irma Serrano. When Madonna was still in diapers, Irma Serrano wrote a book about her sexual exploits, including a love affair with former Mexican president Díaz-Ordaz.

(To begin a look into the Mexican concept of honor from a popular culture perspective, view the classic films of Pedro Infante.)

The machismo inherited from Spain but later transformed into a unique Mexican brand may have been partially influenced by the Moors, who occupied much of the Iberian Peninsula between the years 711 and 1492.

In modern, urbanized Mexico, machismo is no longer automatically accepted as a way of life. Intellectually, at least, an expanding sector of Mexico's male population is confronting the darker side of machismo and democratizing its relations with women. Males no longer feel a socio-psychological obligation to maintain a casa chica, and females increasingly demand a sharing relationship with men based on equality.

FEMINISTS

The cliche of machismo culture suggests that Mexican women, excepting the *soldaderas* and Irma Serranos, are subservient and pliable. Nothing could be further than the truth.

Already during the colonial period, deep within the ornate baroque formalities in the poetry of Sor Juana Inés de la Cruz were innuendos of a woman thwarted intellectually and perhaps sexually as well by baroque colonial conventions.

In 1915, the First Feminist Congress of Yucatán concluded that "women shall be availed of the full potential and variety of facilities to be applied to the same occupations until now discharged by men alone," and other liberating clauses.

While in contemporary United States they debate whether women are fit for combat duty, Mexican *soldaderas* fought in the front lines of the revolution between 1910 and 1920. And it was a Zapatista *soldadera*, comandante Ramona, and not subcomandante Marcos, who led the successful assault and occupation of San Cristóbal in 1994.

In Mexican poetry, feminism emerged in the exquisite work of Rosario Castellanos, and more recent poets and novelists like Elena Poniatowska have expanded the horizon of Castellanos.

Some women who appear most subservient find a way to defend their rights. One night, Lupita watched as her alcoholic, womanizing husband, Manuel brought home his friends from their night of bar-hopping to continue their revelry. The couple's two daughters were sleeping in a bedroom within a few meters of all the "fun."

Manuel ordered Lupita to prepare some *bistek y frijoles* for his friends. It was a display of power, intended to impress his guests (other-directed honor). Lupita was accustomed to such extremes, and would usually find ways to punish her husband once the two were in private. But this time, she did not wait. She grabbed a shovel from the back patio and taunted the revelers until, one by one, they all left.

"Why did you do that in front of my friends?" Manuel groaned.

Many Mexican women like Lupita, accustomed to seeing bad win out over good in their domestic life, find catharsis in *telenovelas* (soap operas), and their written comic-book version, *historietas*, where good eventually defeats the forces of evil. The ultimate effect of telenovelas is one of pacification; women get their revenge through manipulated fiction.

Over a beer, I asked Manuel if he thought Lupita had the same right as he did to seek sexual partners outside of marriage. "Men," he explained, "have a greater appetite for sex. As long as they satisfy their partner and support their family, anything else is fair game. Women have a different role."

Lupita would have preferred to file for a divorce. But economics forced her to remain married. She was a bright but underachieving woman, with none of the job skills called for by the First Feminist Congress of Yucatán; she had given birth to two daughters before she could complete her schooling. During the years I'd visit these neighbors, I never saw Lupita watching a telenovela. It was as if she didn't want to be distracted from planning a way out. She kept busy making money on her own in commercial activities and helping run her husband's business, a sports club.

Manuel had been on his own as a child in rural Morelos. He had worked as a human scarecrow, protecting the fields of his neighbors. He had scraped and clawed his way up from unskilled factory work to a PRI position operating a public market, in which he was able to save up by extorting the venders under his supervision. Once his own business began to thrive, he discarded the other activities.

79

Having known what it was like to not be provided for as a child, Manuel sincerely believed that having adequately supported his wife and daughters was equivalent to paying his dues. The prize was the freedom to fool around outside his marriage.

Lupita, from highland Mexico City, attributed Manuel's drinking and womanizing to the rural *tierra caliente* subculture of his childhood. As long as they were alone, she could make these criticisms with no repercussions. As the years went by, the sarcasm in her critiques sharpened into caricatures of resignation.

When the daughters finished school and Lupita had more free time on her hands, she did to Manuel what he had been doing to her. She found a lover.

With all the casas chicas in Mexico, it is not plausible mathematically that only men take lovers; it figures that a considerable number of women take their destiny into their own hands. Many of them have not had the opportunity to read some of Mexico's fine feminist literature and are acting on the basis of objective reality.

They are today's *soldaderas*, as symbolized by the sister-soldadera in the Alfonso Arau film *Like Water for Chocolate*, who liberates herself from a repressive family tradition.

Some critics would regard film director María Novaro as a feminist, others as simply a skilful *cineasta*. Rent her films *Danzón, Lola,* and *Mambo,* and judge for yourselves.

Curiously, the less-industrialized south of Mexico seems to produce the greatest variety of liberating women's history. The First Feminist Congress (Yucatán), Rosario Castellanos (Chiapas), Comandante Ramona (Chiapas) and matriarchal settlements in the Isthmus of Tehuantepec are all southern phenomena. (State-imposed patriarchal structure on the Isthmus has led to interior conflict within some Tehuantepec women.)

According the Anthropologist Maya Lorena Pérez Ruiz, the field of contemporary Mexican anthropology has shown considerable interest in gender-related research, and the Zapatistas have included

In the D.F. neighborhood of Coyoacán, you'd think you were in an idyllic village and not the most polluted city in the world. Nearby is the former homeof artist Frida Kahlo, now a museum.

gender in their ideological discourse. The strongest currents of feminism are observed among legislators and intellectuals.

Today's symbols regarding the role of women in society seem to have shifted. The most noteworthy of these modern metaphors may be the history of the great mural painter Diego Rivera, whose appetite for women was legendary. Until recently, Frida Kahlo was known primarily as the wife of Diego Rivera, who also happened to be an artist. Today, many consider Frida Kahlo as the greater of the two artists.

In Mexico City's most attractive neighborhood, Coyoacán, with its luxuriant parks, tree-lined streets, colorful colonial facades, and assortment of bohemian cafes, you can visit the Museo Frida Kahlo (Londres 247, at the corner of Allende, north of Plaza Hidalgo, closed Mondays).

81

CHILD LABORERS

In the vicinity of tourist attractions, children may hound you to take care of your car, wash your windshields, shine your shoes, be your guide. Laws against child labor are unenforceable in scenarios where neither parents nor State have the means to provide for children.

Father Homero, from Monterrey, has worked in many countries, including Bolivia, statistically the poorest Spanish-speaking nation in Latin America. This young priest, wearing secular clothing and looking more like a hippie screen star, perceives that poverty in urban slums and depressed rural areas in Mexico is even more demeaning than in parallel locations in Bolivia. If you believe the young priest, then Mexico's large industrial base and laudable gross national product have little or no impact on poverty.

You may dislike the fact that children are out there hustling, but the alternative of begging is worse. Most of these youngsters are bright and amiable, and it is worth hiring them. In a way, you are paying a social tax directly to the beneficiary rather than through a government agency.

We once took in one of these child vagrants, fully aware that life on the streets might win him back. We met the eleven-year-old Pedro after hearing him sing songs on buses in exchange for tips. Pedro told us he had no parents and that he survived on the street.

Pedro faced his first test under our tutelage when receiving money for a haircut. The odds were about even money that he would disappear with the money.

But he returned, his shiny black hair neatly trimmed. At home on the streets, Pedro would have developed cabin fever if cramped in an apartment for too long, so we'd send him on errands. At home, we worked with his reading and writing skills in preparation for the school year. His schooling had been spotty, and the lack of continuity was apparent in his written language skills, although his participation in the street economy had sharpened his spontaneous oral communication and math skills.

One day, Pedro left to do an errand and never returned. Perhaps the ominous prospect of a year in school outweighed the comforts and human warmth of a home. Perhaps he had lied to us and his parents were still alive. Perhaps he was simply lured back by the streets.

The income of some child street laborers goes directly into pockets of their parents, with the child himself receiving few rewards for his labor.

Child guides who hang around tourist sites are sometimes remarkably perceptive and may add a sense of humor to their presentation. These are the elite of the street laborers. On the other extreme are the *tragafuegos* (the fire swallowers), who perform acts that can only result in permanent harm to their health and wellbeing.

In some urban areas, *tragafuegos*, *boleros* (shoe shiners), and other street laborers must pay a commission to the adult who "controls" the turf where they work.

At an early age, through their contact with tourists, many of these children begin dreaming of economic sanctuary in *El Norte*.

THE INFORMAL ECONOMY

Street vendors, independent mechanics like Mario, junk recyclers, automobile caretakers, and other creative hustlers fill a gaping void in the Mexican economy and serve as a safety valve against social convulsion. The classic Ignacio López-Tarzo movie, *El Hombre de Papel* (the Paper Man) is recommended for a quick course on Mexico City street survivalists.

In Torreón, I descended the stairs from an office appointment to discover out on the street that two men had just finished washing and shining my car.

Before I could voice a protest, one of the men explained:

"Sir, we know you didn't ask us to wash your car. But we have no work. We cannot remain idle, even if we must work for free. You don't have to pay us if you don't want to."

Photo: Juan Carlos Vega

A street vendor with a prime location at the foot of Zacatecas stairway.

They had me where they wanted me. How could this Gringo not be impressed by the epitome of the American work ethic! They were generously compensated.

EXILES

As the Mexican diaspora pours out of the country in search of work, Mexico takes in political refugees from the rest of the world.

When Leon Trotsky and his wife Natalia sought refuge from Stalin's death sentence, they moved in with Diego Rivera and Frida Kahlo in 1937. With the reception of Trotsky and other exiles of diverse leftist and libertarian persuasions, president Lázaro Cárdenas established a practice that would continue to the present day.

Governments subsequent to Cárdenas, in the name of the "institutional revolution" would establish a foreign policy that protected dissidents of diverse progressive ideologies and rejected intervention against foreign revolutions.

"Remember when Cuba was punished by the Organization of American States!" proudly declared a Mexican diplomat. "The only country that opposed the measure was Mexico."

Leon Trotsky was murdered by a Stalinist of Spaniard descent in 1940, a second attempt on his life. The great muralist José Alfaro Siqueiros was allegedly involved in the first botched attempt. By then, the Trotskys were no longer living with Frida Kahlo and Diego Rivera. It was an historical period when leftists were obligated to take sides within very narrow ideological parameters, and Diego and Frida evidently disagreed on the proper course. Her biographer wrote that Marxism had given Kahlo the strength to withstand the agony of a life on crutches and in wheelchairs resulting from an excruciatingly painful bus accident that had left her permanently disabled in her teens.

The Trotsky saga was atypical of most exiles welcomed by Mexico. The Mexican government had engineered a type of brain drain in reverse. Typically, poor countries would lose their intellectuals, artists, and technicians to Europe or the United States. But in offering a haven to dissenters from around the world, Mexico was enriching its sciences, arts, and letters.

Republicans from the Spanish Civil War, including poet León Felipe, were the first wave of incoming exiles. Ironically, as the Mexican government fought guerrillas from within, guerrillas from wars in Central America were welcomed as refugees in Mexico.

The story of the great Bolivian muralist and painter, Walter Solón Romero is typical. In the seventies, the southern cone of South America fell under the control of various military dictatorships. The quixotic utopian Solón Romero was a voice in favor of freedom that threatened the established order. His paintings would aggravate military dictators. His sketches entitled *El Quixote y los Perros* (Don Quixote and the Dogs) got him in trouble with uniformed authorities, who interpreted the dogs as symbols of the military.

Walter Solón Romero would lose a son to the Bánzer dictatorship in the 1970s. José Carlos Solón Romero was "disappeared," tortured and executed. With his own life in danger, Solón Romero found refuge in Mexico.

While in Mexico, many of the great Solón murals were decimated by the Bolivian military. Very literally, Bolivia's loss was Mexico's gain. Walter Solón Romero, who had once studied under the great Mexican muralists, would now return as a partner in restoring some of Mexico's great ancient murals, in the company of Mexican restoration experts like Tomás Gaitán.

In his own murals, Solón Romero had experimented with virtually every type of material, a skill that helped him decipher the mysteries of the composition of the murals at the pyramids of Teotihuacán, which included substances from the Mexican nopal.

Today, restorations from Teotihuacán done by Gaitán and Solón Romero may be seen in the Museo de Antropología in Chapultepec forest in Mexico City, as well as in a smaller museum at the site of the great Teotihuacán Pyramids of the Sun and Moon, 50 kilometers northeast of Mexico City.

Teotihuacán was probably the greatest of Mexico's pre-Hispanic cities. Surrounding the pyramids is a green valley dotted with rural villages. Within those villages are makeshift signs outside of rural dwellings that read *pulque* (an alcoholic drink that dates back to the indigenous cultures of the valley). Pulque, made from the sap of the maguey century plant, tastes like punch but includes a delayed detonator. Drinking moderate amounts of pulque and then visiting Teotihuacán can be a time-warping experience. Too much pulque and you might find yourself volunteering for a human sacrifice at the peak of the Pyramid of the Sun.

The frescos at the base of Teotihuacán structures would have been totally eroded under the onslaught of desecration and the abrasive air contamination. With the help of exile Solón Romero, these works of art have been carefully dislodged and restored. The Solón story is a visual metaphor of desecration and restoration: great artists, writers, and scientists violated by their native countries and restored by Mexico.

With democracy on the rebound in South America, Walter Solón Romero and so many other exiles from the world of the arts, sciences, and letters, have bid farewell to Mexico and returned to their native countries, but not before they left indelible imprints on the country that took them in. Other cultural worker exiles have chosen to remain in Mexico, where they find a seductive setting for their work.

In April 1997, three human rights worker refugees, two from Central America and one from the United States, were expelled from Mexico. According to the Federation of International Human Rights Leagues, the three expulsions occurred "in a context of growing repression against the defenders of Mexican human rights."

Since those reports, the son of the man who opened Mexico's doors to social dissenters has now been elected to the second most-powerful position in Mexico: governor of the Federal District. Mexico's tradition as a haven for political rebels has been reaffirmed.

ECONOMIC REFUGEES

Visitors to Mexico driving or busing from U.S. states of California, Arizona, New Mexico and Texas may choose between 20 border crossing cities and towns. Mexican workers crossing in the other direction may find none of these options.

As Mexico's economy becomes increasingly capital intensive, displaced workers in a high unemployment economy have no choice but to take to the road in search of work. Invisible hordes of peasants and townspeople immigrate to Mexico City, to begin hustling from shantytown hovels in search of subsistence. Others take a greater risk and cross illegally into the United States, paying exorbitant fees to *coyotes* or *polleros* (smugglers) or crossing deserts and evading highway roadblocks. They show up in cities like Los Angeles and Chicago or at rural migrant labor camps.

The common perception in the United States is that illegal immigrants, the majority of whom come from Mexico, are taking jobs away from U.S. citizens and residents and draining social service budgets. Advocates for the undocumented workers argue that they are actually beneficial to the U.S. economy, taking jobs no one else wants, injecting wealth into the economy by becoming faithful consumers, not applying for deserved tax refunds out of fear, and using social services to a far lesser proportion than their legal counterparts.

Mexico's foremost expert on immigration is Dr. José Bustamante, Director of the Colegio de la Frontera Norte in Tijuana. Dr. Bustamante says that discussions on clandestine immigration should be based on real statistics on the job market and its laws of supply and demand.

"The main export product of the State of California," he says, "is its agricultural produce, which is equivalent to a third of all agricultural production in the United States. These products come from a labor force that is more than 90 percent Mexican, with 66 percent of that workforce either illegal or irregular."

Referring to 1997 statistics, Bustamante adds that "the demand in the United States for undocumented workers had risen slightly as the supply had slightly diminished."

The new U.S. immigration law, he continues, "has the effect of diminishing the salaries of immigrant workers," because, with harsher sanctions against the immigrants, employers now enjoy a "take-it-or-leave-it attitude" towards prospective employees.

The laws are "making the deportable more deportable, but there are a series of sanctions which signify that the U.S. does not want to close its border; what it wants is to cheapen its workforce. The more they need them [illegal immigrants], the cheaper they want them."

This scenario is derived from what Dr., Bustamante calls "the asymmetry of power between Mexico and the United States. Through xenophobia, they (U.S. politicians) have scandalously converted Mexico and its immigrants into a social enemy."

Flagrant incidents, like the videotaped beating by California police of three Mexican migrants, and the death of another eight after a chase by the border patrol have provoked widespread outrage in Mexico.

But, according to *Guardian* writer Phil Gunson, "Mexico expels more than 70,000 illegal aliens across the Guatemalan border each year," in accordance with Washington's pressure on the Mexican government to keep out the Central Americans.

A survey by the Mexican human rights commission states that 67 percent of illegal migrants from Central America reported suffering "ill treatment, beatings and threats at the hands of the [Mexican] authorities." Amnesty International calls conditions of detained illegal Central American immigrants in Mexico as "inhuman and degrading."

As Mexican diplomats complain to Washington about treatment of undocumented immigrants in the U.S., so do Central American embassies in Mexico complain of human rights violations against Central American immigrants.

Gunson cites estimates that the opening up of Mexican agriculture to foreign competition under the North American Free Trade Act (NAFTA) will drive up to 15 million people off the land by the year 2010.

NAFTA legalized the free movement of capital across borders but failed to consider the free movement of labor as a parallel aspect of free trade.

The Mexican government does little to deter the flight of its desperate job seekers because illegal immigration relieves the pressure for social reform and "remittances from migrant labor represent between $3 billion and $6 billion - more than Mexico's agricultural exports."

Meanwhile, in northern Mexico and the Southwest of the United States, a cottage industry of Tex-Mex music is dedicated to the plight of the undocumented migrant workers, for whom a steady job, no matter how demeaning, represents salvation from desperation and hunger.

One of the great dramas of the end of the twentieth century involves the massive movement of migrants in search of work and sustenance. Mexico is one of the major stages of this drama.

IT'S A BIRD, IT'S A PLANE, IT'S SUPERBARRIOS

Most working class Mexicans never get to El Norte or as some call it, *el otro lado* (the other side). The most unfortunate of these laborers and unemployed become virtual prisoners in unseemly tenements described by anthropologist Oscar Lewis in his *Children of Sánchez*. In these *vecindades*, whole families are confined to cramped quarters, with few common bathrooms, and sinks shared by the multitude.

During one afternoon conflict between protesters and police around the *vecindades* in the historic center of Mexico City, an unlikely apparition arrived on the scene: a man in a cape with an SB inscribed on the chest of his shirt, and a mask over his face. He called himself El Superbarrios. *(Barrio* is defined in Mexico as a working class neighborhood.) He is a cross between comic book superheroes like Superman and Batman, and masked professional wrestlers like *El Santo* (The Saint). A fluid translation of "Superbarrios" to English does not exist.

El Santo and his offshoots belong to a global subculture of professional wrestlers who stage good guy/bad guy rituals. In the United States, in both professional wrestling and superhero comics, the heroes fight the criminal underworld. But it is unheard of for a superhero to confront social issues like inadequate housing, police abuse, and human rights violations. El Superbarrios injects social ideology to the superhero role, fighting oppressors and defending the disenfranchised.

El Santo was an icon in the ring and on the movie screen. This author once took his son to see a card of professional wrestling that included masked heroes in the tradition of El Santo, at an arena in the working class neighborhood of Naucálpan, north of Mexico City. The frenzy among the spectators led to a great catharsis as each match reached a climax. Never mind that it was all a show. I observed the grim living conditions in sections of Naucálpan surrounding the arena and suspected that such theatre served to buffer the effects of harsh reality.

Today's Superbarrios (there are now at least five of them) attempt to change reality, to politicize the tenement dwellers, infusing anti-hero humor to the struggle. From his midriff bulge, you can tell that El Superbarrios has not been sculpted into a mythical-commercial physique.

I asked Mexican anthropologist and author Maya Lorena Pérez Ruiz about El Superbarrios in the context of her three contemporary Mexican cultural paradigms: alienated culture (resulting from commercialization); culture superimposed by a dominant political power; or a truly autonomous culture?

The Superbarrios seems to resemble the alienating figures of professional wrestling, I suggested. Could he represent what you call "alienated culture"?

Pérez Ruiz pondered for a moment, and then responded with proud conviction. "The Superbarrios is an authentic cultural phenomenon."

I then asked Pérez Ruiz to comment on Bartra's denunciations of government attempts to forge a compliant national culture. Referring to the work of the great Mexican anthropologist Guillermo Bonfil Batalla and his *México Profundo*, Pérez Ruiz established a parallel between the urban tenements that engendered El Superbarrios with the indigenous cultures referred to by Bonfil Batalla. The Superbarrios, she commented, has adopted an alienating distortion of popular culture and remodeled it into an authentic manifestation of the most profound sentiments of Mexico's urban disenfranchised.

Mexico City's tenements are the urban equivalent to the indigenous communities of Chiapas, suggests the anthropologist. "In a bizarre way, El Superbarrios is the urban version of El Subcomandante Marcos."

El Superbarrios belongs to what is called the "popular urban movement" and is affiliated with the opposition political party, the PRD (Party of Democratic Revolution), whose candidate Cuauhtémoc Cárdenas was triumphant in the first open election for governor of the Federal District (D.F.).

El Superbarrios typically arrives at Mexico City's large central plaza, El Zócalo, in his equivalent to the Batmobile, *el barriomóvil*, in reality an old truck. There, a makeshift wrestling ring is set up, and mythological matches are fought, with the good guys, El Superbarrios, El Superecologista, El Superanimal, always defeating the bad guy: a corrupt politician, a polluting industrialist, a human or animal rights abuser.

El Superbarrios has slipped into the chambers of Mexico's House of Representatives to raise an issue, and has attempted, unsuccessfully, to meet with President Zedillo.

As Clark Kent fronts for Superman, the original Superbarrios has his civilian name: Juan Carlos Gómez. On one occasion, Gómez arrived on a flight to Los Angeles, California. The airport police spotted a man with a mask, a cape, and an SB on his shirt, not the usual travel apparel. The Superbarrios was arrested by a very suspicious airport police unit.

As more Superbarrios emerge, Mexico proves once again that the same popular culture used by authorities to subdue social consciousness can be turned into a symbol of social justice.

Ever since the muralists of the Mexican Revolution inscribed their defiant messages on public buildings, cultural rebellion has become an inherent part of the Mexican way of life.

YOUTH

Two enormously popular rock music groups document the defiance of Mexico's youth culture. The staunchly eclectic Café Tacuba opposes the status quo of the music industry by refusing to fit in with a commercial niche. This is the first truly mestizo rock group. Café Tacuba does in Mexico what contemporary pop music has been doing in France, mixing both musical genres and ethnic harmonies. Café Tacuba dips into traditional Latin romantic music, salsa, northern Tex-Mex, and of course, rock 'n' roll.

The four young men from Naucálpan who comprise Café Tacuba use the underground language of the *barrio* to highlight their cultural roots, a jargon which sometimes sounds foreign to audiences in other Latin American countries where they tour. The "Tacuba" is a sprawling working class D.F. neighborhood, and Café Tacuba is Mexican, in the broad sense, but also *chilango* (of the Mexico City working class culture).

Lead singer Anónimo (Anonymous), Joselo and Quique Rangel (guitar and bass respectively) and Emmanuel del Real (Keyboard) have created a type of techno-tropical fusion music, covering the whole tonal rainbow between hardcore punk and romantic. Their album RE makes culturally defiant statements about Mexico's youth.

The group Maldita Vecindad (Cursed Tenement) is a bit less eclectic musically but considerably more political in their message. In their own way, they have done what El Subcomandante Marcos and El Superbarrios are doing: using the fascination of masks in popular culture to create a sung poetry that reflects or protests against the disenfranchisement of the working and lower middle classes. Their recording *Baile de las Máscaras* (Dance of the Masks) quotes Mexican intellectuals Octavio Paz and Alfonso Reyes on the jacket. Both Paz and Reyes write about Mexico's contradiction between its apparent and secret identities.

MASKS

El Superbarrios, Maldita Vecindad, and el Subcomandante Marcos don their masks to mirror a social truth, that Mexican society has encouraged the use of an invisible socio-psychological mask to hide painful cultural and historical truths. The mask is an overt admission that the cover-up exists.

"I am prepared to take off my mask," declared Subcomandante Marcos, "if Mexican society will take off its own mask."

Maldita Vecindad traces the Spanish word *máscara* to the Arabic language, and Arabic influence may be perceived in several of the group's compositions.

(The Mexican film *El Callejón de los Milagros*, winner of 32 international awards, portrays the type of Mexico City tenement (*vecindad*) neighborhood that inspired the name Maldita Vecindad. This gripping film critiques machismo, and its plot is traced to Arabic cultures, having been based on a novel by the Nobel Prize-winning Egyptian author Naguib Mahfouz.)

Songs/poems by Maldita Vecindad evoke the poverty of street people (*The Organ Grinder* is especially poignant) and lance direct attacks against the established order. The song *El Dedo* refers to the president's finger that points out his successor. The song *Por Ahí* slams at neoliberal economics and demagoguery; "progress" has not reached six-year-old Lupe, who still must spend her days selling on the streets: "She's angry/it's a long time/500 years of waiting."

Maldita Vecindad's Aldo, Roco, Pacho, Pato, and Sax (masked behind nicknames, and masked on the cover of their recording) are ideological cousins of El Superbarrios. They are pitted in a tug-of-

Photo: Bernardo Peredo

Quique Rangel and Manuel del Real (Meme) of Café Tacuba in performance.

war, trying to snatch popular culture away from those of the power structure who would used it to politically alienate the public. One Maldita Vecindad song *No Les Creo Nada* (I don't believe anything they say), names an important figure of popular culture, Mexico's agile football goalie, Jorge Campos (famous for the flashy sportswear of his own design he uses on the field). The song begins with the following lines, paraphrased from the original:

"Today I learned from the TV that our country is not bad off/with Jorge Campos we can win the World Cup/I don't know who they deceive/our street is not on the TV screen."

No simple cliche can sum up the trends among Mexico's youth. D.F. youth tend to be more anti-establishment and cynical, demonstrating "an unbelief in the political parties," according to anthropologist Pérez Ruiz. Members of the opposition PRD who have risked and sometimes lost their lives in defense of democracy are thought of by some youth as "old hippies." On the other hand, the youth vote was strategic in the Cuauhtémoc Cárdenas victory.

In general, the youth have shown a "double attitude" about the Zapatistas, explains Pérez Ruiz, something like "I agree with you but not with the armed struggle." Unorganized youth thus helped prevent a civil war, with Zedillo winning a legitimate presidential election in part on his position against militarily rooting out the Zapatistas.

More Masks

During an important address to Congress by President Zedillo, an opposition legislator donned a mask: the face of a pig. Ten minutes into Zedillo's speech, PRD Congressman Marco Rascón then calmly walked up to the podium. He set up 25 posters, among them: "Enough, the nation is in danger."

Some legislators frowned in disapproval. Others broke out in laughter. The masked Congressman Rascón then raised another poster: "OINK, OINK", and yet another: "Long Live the nineteenth century," in reference to denunciations that Mexico continues to be a backward country.

Rascón ended his protest with a poster reminding the Congress of the assassination of former presidential candidate Luis Donaldo Colosio.

Masking the mask. Here was an ideal moment for the imagistic medium of television. Yet Mexican Televisa TV cameras remained fixed on the figure of the president. Citizens who depended on television for their information would have had no way to learn about Rascón's masked protest. Just how many layers of superimposed masks must be penetrated in order to reach the bare truth of Mexican reality?

THE BATTLE TO CONTROL POPULAR CULTURE

Maldita Vecindad and Café Tacuba are pitted in a culture clash that reflects Mexico's history since the 1910 revolution: musicians, poets, mural painters defending the independence of their art as the power structure attempts to co-opt them.

As they become famous in Mexico and abroad, their music tours are arranged by the type of global enterprises whose only goal is to capture the largest possible market. Will these groups along with artists in other realms be required to tame their boldness and dilute their message?

To the chagrin of Zapatista leaders, even Subcomandante Marcos becomes an object of commercialization, with an array of products based on his masked figure. If the power structure cannot defeat him militarily, they can try to absorb him into the system. Mayan Zapatista commanders called this an affront to indigenous peasants.

"We no longer want to be exploited like animals in a zoo," said one Zapatista commander named Juan.

In her yet untitled book, Maya Lorena Pérez Ruiz asks whether the National Museum of Popular Culture has been an instrument of the State or a venue of expression for authentic popular culture?

"In modern society," she quotes museum director Guillermo Bonfil, "there are forces which tend to remove popular sectors from cultural initiative and convert them into consumers of and not creators of culture."

The great Mexican anthropologist Guillermo Bonfil was quite aware that as director of a popular culture museum financed by the State, he would need to walk a tightrope between what was acceptable to the government and what was a legitimate expression of popular culture.

The exhibition entitled "We Are Workers" was a case in point. For nearly seven decades, the recently deceased head of the Mexican Labor Confederation, Fidel Velásquez, would create what were known as "cowboy unions," labor organizations that fiercely defended the dominant political party, sending in goons to break up expressions of labor independence. Two years prior to his 1997 death, the then 95-year-old labor padrino declared that "we should exterminate the Zapatistas."

From within the museum staff, there were those who fought for the freedom to use the pejorative term "cowboy union" in the "We Are

Workers" exhibition, a provocation that would have resulted in government intervention. Bonfil believed that "it would be totally irresponsible to launch the museum on a course that would be interpreted as provocation.

"There are people," he added, "who don't care that we are saying things that portray reality but who prefer to fight for the use of certain words like "cowboy union" even though we are portraying the exact same concept with other words."

Mexico has a fertile and evolving tradition of popular culture. The most elite of Mexican literature, art, music, and architecture has been steered by the currents of popular culture.

Visitors to Mexico sensitive to the cultural tug-of-war will learn soon enough to separate the strictly commercial from the profoundly authentic in manifestations of popular culture.

We have now met a few of the characters, both prototypical and unconventional, who have played a role in defining the cultural setting of contemporary Mexico. More characters will be introduced as we survey scenarios of business and social etiquette in the following chapter, and yet others as the plot thickens in Chapters Five and Six.

Chapter Four

SOCIAL AND BUSINESS CUSTOMS

Scene in a Cantinflas movie. Cantinflas (Mario Moreno) arrives at a United States border station, intending to cross to "the other side." The border crossing lies on a parched desert dotted with Mexican nopal and maguey and American sagebrush.

The wooden border gate stands alone like a solitary outpost, the only indication that anything resembling a line separates two sides of the desert, two distinct cultures.

Through the slats in the gate, the border patrol guard checks the immigrant documents and finds them in order. But there is one problem. The guard has misplaced the key to the gate.

Beyond either side of the gate, Cantinflas observes miles of empty desert. The exchange between these two characters is paraphrased.

"Don't worry," Cantinflas grins, pointing to the side of the gate where no barrier separates the two countries. "I'll just walk across over here. You don't need to open the gate."

The border guard frowns:

"You must pass through the gate! That's the regulation."

"But," protests Cantinflas, "I can walk right across here and you don't need to find the key."

"Out of the question," responds the guard. "There are rules. The rules must be followed."

It is not unusual for Mexican movies to caricature the Gringo culture in this way. Although the border guard is stereotyped, he represents what Mexicans perceive as a Gringo extreme: lack of flexibility when dealing with rules and regulations.

If there were one single lesson to be applied to both social and business situations in Mexico, it would be to exercise FLEXIBILITY. By all means know the rules and try to follow them. But in typical scenarios, what happens when the spirit of the rule contradicts the letter of the rule? Cantinflas perceived that the Gringo goes with the letter of the law while the Mexican prefers its spirit.

For this reason, at two in the morning on dark and empty streets, the Mexican driver, after looking both ways, will drive right through a red light.

In this spirit of Mexican mores, we'll review various social and business customs in order to facilitate adaptation to Mexico's ways of life. We are visiting a predominantly *mestizo* country and we shall concentrate on this dominant culture. But bear in mind the words of the great anthropologist, Guillermo Bonfil Batalla, that even beyond those more than 50 indigenous peoples who have conserved their internal cultural cohesiveness, "there are a great quantity of isolated (indigenous cultural) traits that are distributed in diverse ways in distinct urban sectors."

SOCIAL CUSTOMS

Meals

In general, the most substantial meal of the day is *el almuerzo* (lunch), often called *la comida* (the meal). In restaurants, a fixed-price *comida corrida* (lunch on the run) is the best buy, and usually includes soup (called *caldo*), rice or noodles (called *sopa*), beans, and an entrée of beef, pork, poultry, or fish. The main dish is usually bathed in a sauce. Corn tortillas (or wheat flour tortillas in northern states) and a *salsa picante* hot sauce accompanies the meal. You can ask for more sauce and tortillas when needed.

A simple desert, jello or fruit, plus a fruit drink *(tamarindo)* or rice drink *(horchata)* are sometimes included in the fixed price. Bottled soda is not usually part of the formula but may be purchased separately. Tortillas are used like utensils, to pick up the food and sauce.

In smaller restaurants, tipping is not required, but the same standard 15 percent customary tip for larger restaurants is deserved in the smaller establishments as well.

Contrary to other Latin American countries, and perhaps from the influence of the country to the north, many Mexicans eat substantial breakfasts, plates like steak, eggs and beans, with coffee. The dinner hour is the least formal. It is believed in some circles that a large meal at night is harmful to digestion. The *merienda* replaces a full dinner and includes sweet breads and coffee or leftovers from lunch.

Every rule has its contradiction, and Mexicans may be found eating at any and all times until the wee hours of the morning. Some of the hottest food businesses serve clientele coming from the *cantinas* late at night. Eating hours are thus much less formalized than they would be in Europe or other Latin American countries. (See Food in Chapter Seven: Survival Skills.)

Social Gatherings

Are you addicted to arriving on time at social gatherings? Do you refuse to arrive at least a half hour late? Go ahead then! Go catch the host in his bathrobe or hostess in hair rollers. Or worse, interrupt them from rolling around in bed together, or catch them in the middle of a spat. Believe me, you will lose and not save time by arriving at the prescribed hour.

Don't get me wrong. You will meet people who do not abide by the late-is-on-time custom. I had a 4:30 p.m. coffee meeting with Father Homero Elías, the young priest-anthropologist from Monterrey. He arrived at the cafe, huffing and puffing, lifted off his backpack, and checked his watch: 4:29 p.m. "I like to be on time," he said.

Mexican friends visiting the U.S. were quite amused to see the hours for beginning and ending the get-together on the invitation. Mexican invitations do not specify at what hour a social gathering is to end, and why should they? If the event is lively, why should people be pushed out by an artificial time constraint.

Mexican social etiquette is quite varied, but certain standard practices represent the safe path. A gift of flowers from the guest, an alcoholic beverage or in some cases a desert will please the host.

When entering a house with invited guests, male guests kiss the female hostess on the cheek, and female guests allow male hosts to kiss them on the cheek. These kisses are accompanied by a handshake. Sometimes, women will greet each other with a kiss on the cheek and handshake. Men greet each other with an embrace and handshake if they are already regular acquaintances: otherwise, with a handshake.

With ethnic, class, and regional variations, both host and guest should play it safe by observing what others are doing. In more formal settings, the guest should greet each and every other guest already present with at least a hand shake.

In general, large urban settings like Mexico City and Monterrey are less formalized, while smaller cities maintain more traditional customs.

Dress

The safe route is to dress conservatively but informally. The lower the altitude (*tierra caliente*) the less formal the dress. T-shirts and wrinkled jeans will mark you as a tourist in most places. But in the tropics, even presidents wear loose, untucked, embroidered shirts called *guayaberas*.

Within the larger picture there are the typical subcultures, ranging from upscale yuppies to pulque-gulping proletarians. Common sense and basic observation skills will distinguish between the dress codes of one group and another.

ADDRESSING PEOPLE

In formal and semiformal situations, both social and business, Mexicans are quite title-conscious. It is important to memorize the title of the person you have just met. Most college graduates are addressed as *licenciado*, as are lawyers. Professionals in technical fields are addressed as *ingeniero* (engineer). Example: "Buenos días Ingeniero Rodríguez."

In a room full of políticos, just call everyone *Licenciado* and you won't go wrong.

I have been in precarious situations in which Mexicans, stopped by police or military officers, address their accosters with a *mi jefe* (my boss). When in doubt as to the proper title, the standard *señor/ señora/señorita* may suffice, but what if the man you call "señor" is really "doctor"?

Señora designates a married woman while señorita refers to unmarried status. In conservative regions, usually in the rural highlands, señorita means that the young lady remains a virgin. When in doubt, use señorita, especially in hyper-traditional places where conserving one's virginity is considered an attribute.

I once sought an oral history interview with an elderly lady I addressed as "señora."

"Señorita!," she pouted, her honor offended. "I have my place reserved in heaven."

In liberalized modern Mexico, I had stumbled upon a vestige of the colonial past. The occasional anachronism of the woman who remains chaste to preserve her spot in heaven is addressed in the stirring poem by Jaime Sabines called "Tía Chofi" (Aunt Chofi).

Remember that the more traditional the region, the more likely you will use the formal "you" *usted* rather than the informal "you" *tú*. In some rural regions, within the same family, younger members address elders with *usted*, but this custom is dying out. On the other hand, in urban centers, people of the same generation who do not even know each other may use the informal *tú*.

If you've not learned or forgotten a person's title at a formal gathering, the second best solution is to refer to that person with the formal "you" *(usted)*.

Nicknames

The informal *tú* is used for friends, family (except elders in traditional families), regular acquaintances, and same-age casual acquaintances in urban centers and lowland areas. Once you've shifted into the *tú* mode, you may not like what they call you.

North Americans and northern Europeans may be offended when they are addressed according to their appearance, but this is standard practice throughout Latin America.

For example, friends call me *flaco* (skinny) or *guero* (whitey), clearly terms of fondness. If you are black, you may be called *negro* or *negrito* (the *ito* diminutive expresses affection). An overweight person may be called *gordito* (fatty). In English-speaking countries, to be called "fatty" would be a gross insult, but in Mexico and most of Latin America, to nickname a friend or acquaintance on the basis of his/her appearance is an expression of fondness.

"Surely there is some ingredient of offensiveness in such nicknames," I once suggested to a Mexican friend.

"Not at all," he said. "You Gringos are hung up on people's appearance and try to cover up what is simply reality, instead of accepting it."

The honest realism in nicknames seems to contradict allegations by some Mexican intellectuals that their culture hides behind social masks.

Flirting

I once encouraged a student of mine, Joyce, to act on her wishes and go to study Spanish in Mexico. Two months later, I received a letter whose ink was blurred by teardrops. She could not walk more than a few blocks, Joyce wrote, without being hounded by a style of male flirting referred to as *piropos*. The grosser of these *piropos* occurred when Joyce was walking by places like construction sites.

My wife Martha, with a Latin American background but high school and university studies in the United States, believes that *piropos* are usually harmless expressions and that Joyce should have felt honored at best or indifferent if she preferred.

The most common *piropo* typical of Mexico is *"Qué chula!"* or *"Qué chulita"* (how pretty!).

A *piropo* with mild sexual overtones is: *Mamacita!* or with stronger sexual connotation: *Mamazota!*

In modern urban settings, one may now hear women flirting with men, usually when the women are in a group. These flirts are not to be misinterpreted as an invitation to step into bed.

The grosser language that transcends flirting comes from the *pelado* subculture (see introduction). When taking the D.F. metro during rush hours, women should find an all-female car to avoid the possibility of getting pinched by a *pelado*.

Insults

The strongest of Mexican insults are derived from two words: *madre* (mother) and *chingar* (fuck).

A Mexican friend Juan Ramón, was walking near McCormick Place in Chicago, and perhaps because of his light complexion, was mistaken for being Polish by a Mexican at the other side of the street.

"Chingado polaco," said the pelado.

"Polaca tu madre," responded Juan Ramón in Mexican street Spanish, totally surprising his taunter.

Another common male-to-male insult is to call the antagonist "cuñado" (brother-in-law), the implication being that the taunter has slept with the tauntee's sister.

For a foreigner on the receiving end of an insult, the best strategy is to laugh it off, or respond with a sense of humor. Most Mexican insults sound much more menacing than they are, and rarely escalate into physical confrontation.

Accepting a Dare

A male visitor to Mexico may find himself in situations in which his Mexican counterparts wish to see how much tequila he can imbibe. You might be treated to free drinks, as I have been, just so they can see how tough you are at holding your liquor. For me, these situations have always ended harmlessly. Should you remain with your companions (they will be insistent that you do), simply sip slowly, stick with the same drink for each round, and consume food with your drink. If tequila is the drink of the night, ask for a mixed version such as a margarita rather than drinking it straight, or soften the straight stuff by alternating sips between tequila and *sangrita*, a "bloody" concoction of lemon, orange, and tomato juices. Of course, if you are a nondrinker, let your companions know that such beverages are against your religion or against doctors' orders. Hold your ground and they will eventually look for other ways to have a good time.

For a hearty challenge, try the *submarino* (submarine), in which a shot glass of tequila is floated in a larger glass of beer. You go figure how to coordinate this double slugger.

Tequila and Mezcal

These are similar alcoholic drinks. The first is made from the pineapple-like core of a maguey (century plant) called the agave tequilana, whose only natural habitat is the area surrounding the town in Jalisco called Tequila. The latter comes from any number of other maguey plants and a harmless worm is found at the bottom of the bottle.

Dr. José Muriá, historian and director of Mexico's prestigious Colegio de Jalisco in the heart of tequila country, tells us that mezcal is the generic drink from which a variety called tequila was derived. The tequila brand of mezcal was Mexico's first value-added export of the colonial period.

Referred to as mezcal wine, this Jalisco product was not called tequila, according to Dr. Muriá, until 1825, immediately following Mexican independence.

When did they begin drinking tequila with lemon and salt? we asked Dr. Muriá.

"In 1918, an epidemic of Spanish influenza broke out in San Luis Potosí and Zacatecas. The doctors there began prescribing tequila with salt and lemon to flu victims."

Dr. Muriá referred to original documents that attributed a variety of curative powers to tequila, from alleviating the flu to restoring sexual prowess in men over 60.

Why has an alcoholic beverage received a headline in a section on social customs? When tequila and mezcal are drunk straight, there is an elaborate ceremony that takes longer than downing the drink itself. First you lick your hand between thumb and index finger and sprinkle salt on it. Next, you lick the salt and immediately suck on a small green lime, referred to as *limón*, but technically a Persian lime. You then drink the shot in one gulp and lick more salt.

If you don't do it right, no one will ridicule you. I've always done it without the salt. The *limón*, by the way, is also used in beers like Corona and Tecate. For Corona, you actually put the half lime in the

neck of the bottle. With Tecate canned beer, you squeeze the limón on the top of the can and taste it along with the beer.

Once you've drunk beer with a limón flavor enhancer, you'll wonder why you hadn't done it before.

There are three grades of tequila, with the smoother white grade drunk straight without the need for a lemon additive. The darkest tequila is called *añejo* (aged). Beware of street hustlers who may try to sell you a bottle of tequila aged for 10 years for a hefty price. Aging beyond three years will cause tequila to lose its alcohol content.

Dr. Muriá's ample credentials as historian, author, and brilliant teacher cause us to take note when he recommends Tequila Herradura as the only truly pure brand. Sauza and Cuervo, he says, are blended with other alcoholic sources.

The good doctor insists that this product from his home state of Jalisco is superior to the mezcal alternatives, but mezcal is today becoming the BMW among gourmet imbibers, with tequila relegated to Cadillac status.

The best mezcal is produced by Zapotec Indians in Oaxaca, and is bottled with no labels. British alcoholic, consul Geoffrey Firmin, a character in Malcom Lowry's *Under the Volcano*, gave mezcal its first international exposure. Today, it is primitive chic to drink mezcal.

If pitted in a drinking contest, choose the transparent Herradura tequila and you'll increase your lasting power. When Mexicans invite you to drink, they are usually expressing their hospitality, and the drinking contests I've referred to are not commonplace, even though I'd stumble into them regularly.

Hospitality

The most rude of *pelados,* when encountering people in distress, will jump to the rescue, in the tradition of Don Quixote.

While Mexico has its fair share of indifferent people, a large sector of the population seems overly warm and hospitable to foreigners. It took several occasions of asking myself "why is this guy going out of his way for me?" and "what does he want from me?" before I recognized a generous tradition of hospitality in Mexico.

I was returning to Colonia Condesa (Mexico City) from the distant northern suburbs late one night and had to change buses in a tough neighborhood near Azcapotzalco. The second bus I would need to catch was to leave two blocks away from where the first one left me off. My bus driver, knowing that I might miss the last bus of the night, drove his bus two blocks off his route, honked and sped up to catch the other bus after it had departed.

In my country, no matter how generous the bus driver, he would never consider leaving the prescribed route. (Such letter-of-the-law interpretation of regulations is what Cantinflas mocked in the border crossing scene.) In most English-speaking countries, bus company managers would not permit such bending of the rules, while insurance companies would renege on a claim filed from an off-the-route location.

In the interior struggle between opposite Mexican traditions, when romanticism wins out over cynicism, the individual craves for opportunities to do a noble deed. While I do not recommend leaving thousands of dollars in a taxi cab, a Bolivian diplomat who did so was astounded later that night when the Mexico City cab driver returned the money to the hotel where the diplomat was staying, refusing to accept a reward.

On the other hand, cynicism increasingly dominates over romanticism. If a pickpocket is slitting your pocketbook with a shiny knife on a crowded bus, don't expect the other passengers to respond.

Sometimes Mexican earnestness to help extends beyond the brink of reason. When asked directions on the street, some do-gooders prefer to make a guess and give any directions (even incorrect ones) than admit that they cannot be of help. The more labyrinthian the directions, the less likely they'll be valid.

Asking for Help

In extenuating circumstances, the party who goes out of his/her way to help should be offered compensation. Example: the truck driver who stops to pull your car out of a ditch.

In general, the closer people are to their rural roots, the more likely they are to respond to a call for help. I recall driving a wonderful elderly woman named Lolita from Mexico City to Morelia, an eight hour trip, much of it hairpin turns. The lunch hour was beckoning. The eating holes along the way, with decor consisting of free calendars of scantily clad commercial models taped to barren plaster walls, did not appeal to Lolita.

She suggested that we eat in someone's private dwelling, a proposition totally foreign to my own upbringing, where one's home is a bastion of privacy not even accessible to door-to-door salesmen. She looked at the adobe compounds in the wooded foothills above the winding road until she chose one particular home:

"There!," she pointed. "There they have good food."

I drove off the paved road and up a reddish dirt path to our targeted house.

Lolita knocked on the door. A woman in a *chal* answered, "*En qué les podemos servir?* ("How can we serve you?")

"Do you have any extra food today," Lolita asked. There was no

110

mention of money. Evidently it was understood that we would pay for our food.

Our home-made lunch, rice, beans, a meat in a dark sauce, and tortillas, was superior to anything we'd have found in a roadside restaurant.

On a later occasion, I tried the same tactic and happened upon an outdoor rural wedding party where they were serving my favorite dish: chicken in *mole* (a brown sauce coming from pre-Hispanic times made with two types of crushed chile peppers, sesame, garlic, onion, nuts, and chocolate).

Not only were we invited to eat, but the hosts refused to accept payment for the grand banquet.

A Treasure of the Sierra Madre. When driving once through the Sierra Madre Occidental in Chihuahua, over rough, unpaved ranch roads, the inevitable flat tire and the lack of anything resembling a tire outlet, provoked a queasy feeling of vulnerability. An hour later, the spare tire flattened as well.

I wondered whether I'd have to hitch to Chihuahua, purchase a tire, spend the night, and hitch back up into the unmarked ranch roads, praying all the way that my Chevy would still be there.

A passing truck driver took me to the nearest town, where the sole tire distributor did not have my tire size. The townspeople directed me to the local doctor. "Since when do doctors fix flats," I wondered.

With a friendly smile, the doctor lent me a spare tire of his own, a slightly different size, and told me to leave that tire at a particular auto dealership in Chihuahua, where he'd pick it up during his weekly trip to Chihuahua. In an age marked by the disappearance of general practitioners, here was a rural doctor who cured a case of anxiety with one dose of an old tire.

With escalating urbanization and devastating devaluations, traditional Mexican hospitality is under siege. Seasoned travelers report an increasing indifference. However, if there were any place in the world where I'd choose to be if I were in an emergency and needed a generous helping hand (the kind that bends the rules), I'd still choose Mexico.

This is a subjective opinion shared by many other observers of Mexican life, but not everyone has enjoyed similar positive experiences.

Unplanned Encounters

Juan José Arreola's short story/ad "Baby H.P." introduces a new product, made in Illinois, an elaborate harness that, if connected to your hyperactive infant, will collect enough electricity to light your house and run appliances. Rumors of electrocuted babies are highly exaggerated.

Arreola's satire perceives North Americans as valuing practical solutions over human ones. It is the old stereotype that those from the north are cold and calculating while those from the south are passionate and spontaneous.

This largely inaccurate stereotype cannot be totally dismissed. If two friends from so-called northern cultures meet by chance while on their way to errands, they are likely to shake hands, perhaps embrace, and then rush on to their business with a "let's talk on the phone and plan to get together."

In Mexico, the two are more likely to abandon their pressing errands and set off for the nearest cafe or bar. This is not to say that a Mexican doctor will forget about the operation he is scheduled to perform in fifteen minutes, but if the task can wait, the Mexican is apt to let it wait and extend a chance encounter into a meaningful reunion.

Cosmopolitan Mexicans living in the United States relate their amazement at how so many North American friendships are held together by planned meetings while Mexican friends may spontaneously drop by to say hello or ask for help.

"I find it surprising," said Juan Ramón, "that we who come from a culture of many more formalities are much less formalized in the way we sustain a friendship."

This may all change as modern technology and pragmatism acquire a larger determining role in how we use our time.

Oral and Written Formalities

"Northern" cultures tend to get to the point much faster than in a "southern" culture like that of Mexico. Both letters and conversations in Mexico are prefaced by obligatory inquiries as to the health and wellbeing of the person addressed and that person's family.

Conversation protocol in "Latin" countries like Mexico requires speakers to avoid comments that, while well-intended, might be injurious to the companion. Mexicans may see people from "northern" cultures as too blunt and lacking in civility.

The knack is in sensing the subtle boundary between truthful comments and unnecessarily blatant remarks. Good friends may address serious personal and social issues head-on but bypass smaller issues that might be offensive. Lolita explained to me that "God accepts a *mentira piadosa" (pious* lie) when the truth will be more injurious than beneficial.

When invited to a restaurant, if the food is not particularly tasty (to you), why offend the person who invited you with what you consider an objective commentary on the cuisine? In Mexico, some issues are too small to bother with, especially when they might offend a companion.

RURAL AND URBAN

With Mexico's significant rural heritage, many traits that appear to be "cultural" in a national sense are more objectively linked to the rural heritage of the individual.

In general, Mexico's city dwellers are less removed from their rural heritage than their counterparts in other industrialized countries.

The Gringo, says one Mexican *corrido* song, knows of the tomato on his plate but does not know that it had to be picked and sorted.

This writer was taught how to slaughter chickens by a *chilango* (a typical Mexico City resident known for his inveterate urban ways),

and introduced to urban agriculture by another D.F. city dweller. In urban conversations, themes rooted in the rural are much more likely to be prominent in Mexico than in similar industrialized nations where the rural heritage has been forgotten or subdued.

México Profundo

Some apparently rural traits in urban dwellers may emanate from indigenous roots, and a reading of anthropologist Guillermo Bonfil Batalla's *México Profundo* will help you to make such distinctions. I hear the voice of the late Bonfil chiding me that too many of my pages are describing what he calls "México imaginario" (imaginary Mexico). A dominant but minority sector of the Mexican population, he wrote, "is organized according to the norms, aspirations and purposes of Western civilization that are not shared (or are shared from a distinct perspective) by the rest of the population."

My pragmatic approach, Dr. Bonfil, is predicated on illustrating to visitors what they will confront in dominant Mexican settings, be they just or unjust settings, authentic or masked. In the same way that you discover the subtle imprint of the indigenous even in urban customs, I feel, in other customs, reverberations of a medieval Spain that found a second life in the Americas.

What better scenario to appreciate the complex interaction of the Indigenous, the Mestizo, and the Spanish than in Mexico's grand festivals.

LA FIESTA

Does the fiesta reflect an annual opportunity for Mexicans to shed their socio-historical masks and reveal their uninhibited truths, or is it simply a universal craving of all peoples for an annual release from the pressures of daily life?

In Mexico the fiesta is subjected to sociological analysis much the way the game of baseball in the United States catalyzes a profusion of interpretations by sociologists, philosophers and political pundits.

The truth about Mexican festivals is probably perceived more profoundly in a sensorial way, through experience. What is evident is that Mexican and other Latin American festivals are frequent and intense. Every locality, from rural regions to city neighborhoods, has its own patron saint, to be honored with an annual festival. The prototypical festival is a fusion of indigenous and Catholic rituals, promulgated by colonial priests as the most expedient and least convulsive strategy to implant Catholicism.

The fact that so many of these festivals are religious in origin does not preclude, in the more contradictory cases, manifestations of eroticism and hedonism.

Most festivals are linked to the local patron saint, and some Mexicans still celebrate the day of the saint they were named after with more devotion than the day they were born.

Those festivals not associated with a particular place on the following calendar are national in scope.

February

Carnaval. Pre-lent nine-day festival, beginning in late February or early March, famous in Brazil and New Orleans, Louisiana, is a major event in Mérida (Yucatán), Mazatlán (Sinaloa), and especially Veracruz. Carnaval features parades, childrens' shows, artisans' booths, concerts, and fireworks, but here in the tropics, dancing is the main participatory event. Most typical are *Tierra Caliente* dances of

Afro-Latino origin: samba (Brazil), so-called "salsa" (Cuba and the Caribbean), and cumbia (Colombia).

April

Feria de San Marcos. More charro movies refer to the Feria de San Marcos in Aguascalientes than any other annual festival. Three weeks starting in mid-April, with a great parade on Saint Mark's day, April 25. Free musical events, cockfights, *charreadas*, bull fights, and lots of drinking, eating, and dancing. This festival is honored by the classic mariachi song, "La Feria de San Marcos."

Semana Santa (Holy Week), the week leading up to Easter, is vacation time in Mexico. A few of the most colorful versions of this celebration are found in smaller places like San Miguel Allende or Pátzcuaro. Semana Santa exemplifies Mexico's unique blend of the religious and the secular.

May

Cinco de Mayo. Mexico's victory over the French on May 5, 1862 in Puebla was the first time that an "American" army defeated a European invader. Although Puebla is the focal point of this festival, Cinco de Mayo is celebrated wherever Mexicans live, from Chiapas to Chicago.

Corpus Cristi. Papantla, Veracruz, on Highway 180. Last week in May, with the featured procession on the first Sunday of the festival. Huasteca dances like Los Huehues (old men) and Los Negritos are preludes to the main attraction, *Los Voladores* (the flyers). Five men in vibrant festival outfits climb to the top of a high pole. The fifth man performs an overture dance from a platform atop the pole as he plays a whistle and drums. The other four then leap off backwards into the air, each from a rope. They revolve around the pole, descending slowly as their ropes unravel. Each *volador* circles the pole 13 times, for a total of 52 revolutions, 52 being an important number in modern and pre-Columbian calendars.

Photo: Roberto Gaudelli

Oaxaca Fiesta: the streets come alive with dancing.

117

July

Guelaguetza, Oaxaca. The first two Mondays after July 16, this is one of Mexico's most extravagant yet authentic festivals of indigenous dances, highlighted by the Papaloapan women's pineapple dance and the Zapotec feather dance, a symbolic re-enactment of the Spanish conquest of Mexico. Held in the amphitheatre on Cerro del Fortín. Indigenous dances of Oaxaca are seen in less formal settings during patron saint festivals of smaller towns and villages.

September

Independence Day. On September 16, guerrilla priest Hidalgo's "Grito de Dolores" is celebrated with general revelry and political demagoguery throughout the country. At El Zócalo plaza in Mexico City, the unwary may get hit with eggs or other harmless weapons. The town of Dolores Hidalgo, where Hidalgo first shouted "Death to the Gachupines," is the most historically valid site to celebrate.

Twentieth century proponents of the "Theology of Liberation" may find inspiration in Father Hidalgo, who sponsored study groups of banned books, questioned the authority of the pope, and had a mistress. It was against human nature as God created it, he said, for men to be celibate. Hidalgo, an intellectual criollo steeped in the ideas of the Enlightenment, was executed by his own for having allowed the Indian hordes to play a major role in his insurrection.

October

Fiestas de Octubre. Guadalajara's month-long bash, includes the arts (free concerts), agriculture (livestock shows), sports, and on another tier, religion (the procession of the Virgin of Zapopan). Free entertainment at many venues throughout the city.

Festival Internacional Cervantino. Guanajuato. This event was inaugurated as a celebration of the work of the author of *Don Quixote de la Mancha*, Miguel de Cervantes, and has developed into one of the world's great arts festivals, with art, music, dance, theatre, and historical re-enactments. For tickets, inquire at the nearest Mexican Government Tourism Office.

November

Day of the Dead (*Día de los Muertos*). On November 2, the faithful will celebrate the lives that were led by the dead ones in their families. Part of the heritage of this festival comes from ancestor worship in indigenous cultures. The faithful visit cemeteries and share gifts, candy, food and flowers with their deceased loved ones. Candy in the form of human skulls and skeletons is consumed in cemeteries and other venues. The festive atmosphere, according to some specialists, relates to a view of death not as an ending but as another stage of life. The dead come alive in statuettes of skeletons, one of the most unique branches of Mexican artesanry. (Lake Patzcuaro, Michoacán is one of the more noteworthy venues of this national festival.)

20 de Noviembre. More of an historical ritual than a festival, every city has a street named after this date: the break-out of the Mexican Revolution.

December

Day of Our Lady of Guadalupe. Mexican's national Virgen de Guadalupe allegedly appeared on December 12, 1531 before a humble Indian peasant by the name of Juan Diego, conveniently arriving to expedite the religious aspect of the Spanish conquest of Mexico. The focal point for this national festival is the impressive Basílica de Guadalupe in Mexico City. For soul-redeeming penitence, join the pilgrimage on your knees and scrape forward until the cobblestones are streaked with your blood.

Las Posadas. From December 16 leading up to Christmas eve, candlelit processions of both adults and children dramatize the journey of Mary and Joseph to Bethlehem. These processions go from

On Day of the Dead the lives of deceased loved ones are celebrated. A whole branch of Mexican artisanry is based on this festival.

house to house, with escalating festivities, culminated with the breaking of a *piñata*, a colorful papier-maché figure stuffed with candy and coins. (Piñatas are also a birthday tradition.) The children are blindfolded, and one by one given a chance to swing a bat or pole against the piñata. Some piñatas are complex works of artisanry taking many hours to make, only to be broken and lost forever. When the piñata breaks, the children rush in to grab as many goodies as they can.

Smaller festivals. Hundreds of festivals in smaller towns are less structured and sometimes more frenetic, which may be of greater interest to the seasoned Mexican traveler who seeks something different. When traveling to a particular region, check in advance with the Mexican Government Tourism Office for an updated calendar of regional festivals.

BUSINESS CUSTOMS

Having operated my own small business in Mexico and been an official Spanish-English interpreter for bilateral encounters between Mexican and U.S. industrialists, I should have managed to decode the nuances of business communication. Yet business in Mexico remains, for me, an open-ended subject.

In the following pages, important answers to business concerns will be provided, but for the most part we shall let the anecdotes speak for themselves.

Middleman Heritage

Three hundred years of colonialist structures still leave an imprint on how business is conducted in contemporary Mexico. The term mestizo, originally referred to as a mixed racial identity, is here used strictly in cultural terms.

Throughout the colonial period, mestizos were used by the colonizers as middlemen. Employed as police, foremen, and local political bosses, they were taught to consider themselves above the indigenous cultures but below the European. (See Eric Wolf's poetic *Sons of the Shaking Earth*, University of Chicago Press, 1959, a comprehensive analysis of Mesoamerican mestizo history that probably leans too far on the side of cultural determinism.)

Post-revolutionary governments in Mexico created laws which permitted foreign entrepreneurs to own no more than 49 percent of an enterprise. But an astute shareholder with far less than 49 percent can control a company.

The 49% law engendered a class of Mexican businessmen, in the middleman tradition imposed by Spanish colonialism, called *prestanombres* (name-lenders). A foreign interest could dominate a business by simply paying name-lender fees to those Mexicans who fulfilled the role of native shareholders.

121

Spanish Heritage

The Spaniards themselves brought medieval and pre-capitalist customs to the Americas. They failed to grasp the value of human capital, overworking their peasants, miners and artisans, often to death. They ignored the concept of value-added products, instead exporting raw materials directly to Europe. The economies of Spanish American countries or regions were thus based on the exportation of single crops; had you suggested the model of regional self-sufficiency, the colonizers would have branded you a subversive. Why grow food cheaply in rich mining areas when you could bring it in expensively?

Those in Europe who elaborated the raw materials made more money than those who extracted them from the ground. Gold was exported, but the one who gained a greater profit was he who converted it into jewelry.

Not until the mid 1800s did Mexico's political class acquire the notion that such archaic economic processes were thwarting the economy. Benito Juárez and other "liberals" in the mid-1800s initiated the long process of implanting capitalist production in Mexico. The mechanics of capital growth were understood, but for the most part, political leaders did not realize that the "economic culture" could be changed only through a profound disruption in customs and habits.

Fast forward to the 1990s, and we see Mexico applying neo-liberal economic theories in the context of a global economy. The question is, can a country like Mexico spot its competition a lead of several centuries and still catch up? Opponents to neoliberal policies believe that this is not possible, and that a Mexican business class left without any State support will be engulfed by foreign competition.

Neoliberals respond that Mexico's traditional state enterprises were plagued by corruption and thus, the only alternative is orthodox free market enterprise. Ironically, the very European and North American enterprises that provide the model for orthodox free market enterprise are heavily subsidized by the State. Could U.S. grain, dairy, or defense industries survive without massive government subsidies?

Yet under neoliberal principles, Mexican enterprises (with strategic exceptions like the state-operated oil company, Pemex) are expected to lift the country out of poverty with no state supports.

This author offers no answer for the dilemma, but one particular anecdote illustrates the colonial/middleman business heritage. Back in the seventies, when Mexican companies still produced their own light bulbs, I was called upon to act as Spanish-English interpreter at an O'Hare Airport hotel meeting in Chicago between General Electric officials from the United States and G.E. representatives from Mexico.

My translation was essentially instructions from U.S. G.E. reps. Their Mexican counterparts were told to contact Aurerá department store representatives and warn them that if they continued to sell light bulbs manufactured by other companies, G.E. would withdraw its bulbs from Aurera shelves.

G.E. could win the war with Mexican light bulb companies since it received special tax breaks for doing business abroad. The Mexican state could hardly afford to help its own manufacturers to the same extent, lacking the tax base that existed in the United States.

North-South

Such historical constraints have not deterred a capitalist class from developing in the north of Mexico, centered around Monterrey.

In the south, where indigenous communities abound, semi-feudal economic relationships have persisted. Northern peasants, when displaced by multinational agribusiness, either migrate to the metropolis, take low-paying industrial jobs where they are, or cross the border illegally.

In the south, peasants and crafts-people do not have El Norte nearby as an escape valve, nor is there an industrial infrastructure that can absorb them as cheap labor.

Why do so many countries, Mexico included, divide into an industrialized north and a rural south? Many manufacturing industries in northern Mexico, however, fulfil needs of more northerly post-industrial countries that shun the consequences of industrial pollution and demanding labor forces.

The same industry that would have meant progress in Mexico during the first two thirds of the twentieth century now primarily serves the economic needs of post-industrial countries. Some of the *maquiladoras* at or near the border cities are the most blatant example; U.S. industries export sections of their operations just south of the border to avail themselves of what *Guardian* analyst Phil Gunson calls "dubious employment practices," affecting a largely female labor force.

Employers regard females as more docile and submissive than men. The only problem is that they may fall pregnant. To prevent women from concealing pregnancy at one maquiladora, "the management sometimes obliged the workers to produce their sanitary towels each month to prove they were menstruating," according to Gunson, who cites stories of unpaid overtime and sexual harassment.

Foreign entrepreneurs with creative business ideas that transcend the gloomy paradigm above will be welcomed. Produce value-added rather than neo-colonial exports. Nurture productive forces. Find new markets for old products. Develop partnerships with innovative Mexican businessmen who are constrained only by a lack of capital. Create bioregional business that learns from and promotes indigenous communities.

Regional Vitality

Globalism may be an inevitable business trend but there are serious questions as to the ultimate benefits of a one-dimensional global economy in Mexico. For one, Mexico's fertile tourism industry depends on local and regional variations for its sustainability. Is it mere coincidence that the regular and punishing devaluations of the Mexican currency have occurred in synchronicity with the escalating globalization of the Mexican economy?

B. Traven's short story "Mass Production," anticipated the contradictions of such an economic transition. A brief paraphrase of the story's concept will illustrate a fundamental culture shock in the realm of business.

A North American businessman traveling in southern Mexico is taken aback by the beauty of a Mexican artisan's baskets and immediately thinks of the immense business potential. He asks for the price, and the artisan responds something like 10 pesos.

The entrepreneur asks what that price would be if he purchased five of the same piece. The price is reduced to 9 pesos per item. The Gringo counters with an offer to buy 20, and the Mexican obliges by reducing the price to 8 pesos per unit.

It is then that the North American asks for a price based on an order of a thousand copies of the same piece. He is thrilled by the guaranteed profits that will come with an inevitable reduction in price based on a high-volume order.

In that case, the artisan responds, I would have to charge you 20 pesos per basket.

What? says the Gringo, incensed. If you charge only 10 pesos for one piece, how could you raise the price for such a large order.

Simple, says the artisan. For me to produce such a large quantity, I'd no longer be able to make the items myself. I would be obligated to hire laborers, and train them to do it the way I do. But I would have to use machinery that would make it more difficult to achieve the same quality. I would have to change my whole way of living in order to supply your demand.

Here is the story of a small Mexican producer confronting the tentacles of the global economy, long before globalism became a household issue. Traven's foreign entrepreneur never recovered from the culture shock of his encounter with the basket maker.

Readers considering an entrepreneurial adventure in Mexico will delight in getting to know the following quirks of Mexico's business culture. A brief but handy guide on how to set up a business in Mexico will complete the chapter.

Family Business or Corporation?

The Instituto Technológico y de Estudios Superiores de Monterrey (ITESM), with 26 campuses across the country, creates a business curriculum that reflects a firm conviction. Mexican businesses, according to the ITESM program, are often constrained by their strong family structure. What is needed is a transformation from the limiting family base to a more formal business sense, and a greater vision towards the concept of enterprise.

The ITESM philosophy questions the practice of dipping into business reserves to help out family member or close friend in need. I met one businesswoman who had lost three retail businesses after she'd lent groceries to destitute townspeople.

The choice between these two extremes in business culture, the corporation and the family/community enterprise, is the great dilemma for traditional cultures transitioning into a global economy.

Fortunately, there are other themes within the business arena with less agonizing consequences.

The Art of Waiting

I was once employed as an interpreter for a group of California industrialists visiting their counterparts in Aguascalientes, on a three-day trip. I fully expected that, by the third day, I would be translating concrete business agreements.

I was wrong. Throughout the three days and nights, the primary purpose was to establish rapport. During a lunch at the luxurious estate of one of the Aguascalientes entrepreneurs, I was called upon to sing a few Mexican ranchera songs as I strummed the guitar. For performing this simple act, I was considered a hero by my U.S. employers. What they wanted was to fit in, to leave their new Mexican acquaintances with a sense that they came in good will.

Eventually, joint enterprises did develop, but not before a prolonged period for the accumulation of trust and rapport. Many of the conversations I translated had to do with family, sports, and vague economic issues. Entrepreneurs of one country would describe how their business functioned to their counterparts from the other country.

The Soft Sell

My own humble business involved English and adult education classes for factory workers and secretaries, paid for by their employers. I would approach personnel managers or human resource directors, and propose a concept. It would be in the best mutual interest of company (positive industrial relations) and employees (self-actualization) if the company were to finance courses of study for their employees.

The soft sell seemed to work much more effectively than the hard sell, provided that it was accompanied with nuances of great self-confidence on my part. I knew that my proposal itself was solid, but I came away understanding that contracts were obtained because of the rapport I had established, and the patience and serenity of my presentations.

Personal Communication

Much of the world is passing through an historical period in which written culture supersedes oral culture and technology displaces personal contact. Mexico is a technologically advanced country that also produces first-class written literature.

Yet, it is very difficult to get things done via written documents and technological communication alone. Personal contact is a must for surmounting hurdles in a country where even the most fervent urban zealots are not far removed from a rural past.

In order to establish such personal contact, a letter or phone call from an important person is of great help. However, opening doors to new opportunities depends less on what you have accomplished, as outlined in your letter, and more on whom you know.

Along the way, you will inevitably have to deal with a typical Latin American prototype: the frustrated and underpaid bureaucrat whose only way to feel important is to hold you back. When dealing with this character, the best strategy is to act important, and if possible, to show that you have the backing of other people who are more important than you are. A firm but not overly forceful handshake, a smile exuding confidence, and clean-cut, conventional dress, not overly formal, will also help pave the way. Fortunately, these bureaucrats are not the ones who will be involved in final agreements.

Once personal rapport has been established with the party with whom you intend to open business channels, written and technological communication then acquire greater significance. But in the initial stages of the process, personal communication is essential.

Cultivating Business Contacts

The greatest error in ongoing business with Mexicans is to go straight to the point without first appreciating other aspects of the person you are dealing with.

Business relations are typically cultivated over lunch. During initial lunches, table talk tends to evade business themes. Your knowledge of professional football/soccer standings, popular culture, and current events is a helpful bridge in communication. Mexican current events in particular often have close links with larger historical concepts.

Mexicans and Latin Americans in general are often interested in your family. When you are perceived as part of a family, your alien shell is dismantled.

Manners, including graciousness and attire, are valuable assets in a business relationship. In general, dress is more formal in highland areas, and less formal in the lowland tropics, where, we repeat, an embroidered *guayabera* shirt, untucked, may replace a sport jacket and tie.

Language

In Mexico, more than in other Latin American countries, an awareness of popular culture, including idiomatic expressions, is a great asset. This results from official post-revolution promotion of a "national culture." Even if business is conducted in English, some knowledge of Spanish is strategic for establishing rapport. An attempt to speak Spanish, even a broken version, is widely applauded.

A primer on basic Spanish structures is found in the Survival Skills section of this book, but at this juncture it is important to highlight that there are two forms of addressing others, the formal and the familiar. The formal "you" *(usted)* is used when addressing people who are neither friends, relatives nor daily acquaintances, and as a sign of respect when addressing elders. The informal "you" *(tú)* is reserved for friends, relatives and daily acquaintances, as well as for people of the same age and generation.

In general, Mexicans are quicker to use the *tú* form than other Latin Americans or Spaniards, especially in urban areas and among people of the same generation. Rural areas remain more traditional in language-related customs.

TIP: if you are addressed in the *tú* form you should respond in kind or it will construed as a put-down, unless the person addressing you is very much your elder. If your business acquaintance says "vamos a tutearnos" it means that the two of you have reached the point at which you know each other well enough to speak on an informal basis. If this is the case, immediately discard the *usted* form.

Personal Service

It seems there are two contradictory business cultures in Mexico. The first, in more traditional settings, provides superb personal service. When times are hard, regular clients get goods on credit. The owner is there personally to see to the customer's every need.

But the opposite exists. "We went into the restaurant and they acted as if we didn't exist," said my daughter Siomara. "We could have gotten up and walked out and they wouldn't have cared."

A *Newsweek* article (September 18, 1995) calls such indifference "a traditional bane of Mexican companies." The success story of entrepreneur Carlos Nakash's Fotos Manhattan provides a positive model. With his company on the brink of collapse, the photo shops altered their modus operandi, peddling discounts, free film, and less-than-an-hour developing: in other words, improved service. Nakash displays his home phone number inside the stores for customer complaints, and his wife personally delivers late orders to customers' homes. With these service improvements, the business catapulted.

It seems as if personal service, a trademark of traditional Mexican culture, had been falling by the wayside as the country modernized, leaving a profitable void for those who would treat their customers with dignity.

A Synthesis of Traditional and Contemporary

Productos Orgánicos del Cabo is a prizewinning company that conjured up the perfect synthesis between the thesis (traditional) and the antithesis (contemporary). In the realm of the traditional, this exporting enterprise has worked closely with traditional communal landholders, called *comunidades ejidales*, in Baja California Sur.

The connection between traditional farmers and contemporary taste is the market niche that seeks organically grown products. The company motto is: Healthy Earth, Healthy Plants, Healthy People.

The enterprise has found willing markets in the United States, Canada, England and Japan.

As modern technology wields increasing influence over contemporary life, some disillusioned sectors of society seek out traditional ways as an alternative. These sectors form a willing market for the types of humanizing products that can still be produced in countries like Mexico, where traditional ways don't fade away.

Other Business Tips
- Do not schedule back-to-back meetings. Business meetings often extend beyond the prescribed time period.

130

- Folks from the United States and even Europeans often use the term "America" when referring to the United States. Don't commit this error; Mexicans are from the Americas and technically are also *Americanos*.

- Business bribery is associated with Mexico, even though it's a universal custom. In Mexico the bribe is called *La mordida* (the bite), but when engaged in a mordida, you never use the word. When an important step in a business process is just not materializing, a bribe may be expected. But confident patience or better yet, a letter from an important person, can get you through the step without paying a mordida. Only as a last resort should you be willing to contribute an extra "service charge."

- If you need a lawyer, ask your country's embassy to recommend one. An unrecommended lawyer may be working for both sides.

- From my own modest business dealings, I come away with a subjective impression; the most successful people in the social nuances of business are those who can walk the fine line between first acting/looking important and then being willing to show glimpses of their vulnerability. Wanted: a character whose self-confidence and aura of importance are so thorough that he is not afraid to bare his weaknesses. Mexico is complex in this way. It is a deceptively informal country in which the same man who "opens up" over a few beers will later back off and behave more privately.

SETTING UP A BUSINESS

The 51 percent Mexican ownership requirement has now been eliminated for the vast majority of business categories. Of the 754 categories of business activities, only 47 remain restricted: either reserved for the State, for ownership of Mexican nationality, or with limitations on foreign participation.

Reserved for the State are all petroleum-related industries, energy (nuclear, electric), telegraph/radiotelegraph, mail, emission of paper and coin currency, and port/airport management.

Activities that require Mexican ownership are land transport, including passenger and cargo (excepting messenger and courier service), fuel distribution, mass media (excepting cable TV), credit unions, development banks, and legal services.

Activities that limit the percentage of foreign ownership include national air transport, businesses operated by financial institutions, stock brokerages, bonding institutions, warehousing, currency exchanges, arms manufacture, national journalistic enterprises, Cable TV, telephone companies, and various types of credit institutions.

Should you be involved in either a restricted or an unrestricted business category, your five best sources of information for getting started are: the Ministry of Trade and Industry (SECOFI), the Mexican Investment Board (MIB, with a Digital Information System at your service), Mexico's Foreign Trade Bank (BANCOMEXT), Nacional Financiera (NAFIN), and Mexico's worldwide network of embassies and consulates. (For addresses /phones /faxes, see "Business Contacts" in the STRATEGIC DIRECTORY at the end of this volume.)

The umbrella organization in charge with directing paperwork (red tape?) for authorizing your business is the Comisión Nacional de Inversiones Extranjeras (CNIE). Technically, if your business is valued at less than 13 million dollars or if you do not hear from CNIE within 45 work days of your petition, your petition should be automatically approved.

But once your business has been approved by CNIE, you must navigate through a labyrinth of government offices. The rough chronological sequence is: Secretaría de Gobernación, Secretaría de Relaciones Exteriores, Public Registry, Inscription in the National Registry of Foreign Investments, the Secretarías of Environment and Health, and the Mexican Institute of Social Security. When adrift within the bureaucratic sea, take the advice of my writer friend Ray Oldenburg and consider waiting time as positive "decompression." Be psychologically prepared for a "please come back tomorrow."

Current regulations prevent this whole procedure from taking more than 133 work days. (It probably took a government bureaucrat 133 days to come up with that number.) Cut down the waiting period considerably if CNIE authorization was not required. According to Bancomext's *Basic Guide for the Foreign Investor*, following the public registry stage, you may begin renting an establishment, installing telephone lines, and opening business bank accounts.

"But sir," you say as you dream of long, dark government corridors. "I'm already paying rent on my business establishment. Surely there must be a way to quicken the procedure."

"Perhaps we can help," says the man behind the desk, thinking *n*ow we've got him. "A supplementary fee of *xxx* pesos will expedite your application."

In the good old days, one could accelerate the process with "supplementary fees" to a few well-chosen people along the way. (This author once employed a taxi driver to take care of such red tape. Naturally, the driver received his commission, but I was thus liberated to stroll through Chapultepec, visit art galleries, bet on the horses at Hipódromo de las Américas.)

In today's more transparent business climate, and with some unfortunate souls doing time on corruption convictions, the best advice is to make the most of your waiting period by nurturing business connections and getting a feel for the avenues of commerce you plan to pursue.

Deregulation. As you wait for approval of the next step in your paperwork, think about how it used to be before deregulation. In pharmaceuticals, for example, there was a waiting period of approximately three months for SECOFI to approve your product price list. Today, companies send price lists to SECOFI and no additional approval is required.

In mining, the Foreign Ministry used to have 45 working days to review applications to set up new firms. Today, Foreign Ministry review must be completed in five working days! In the automotive industry, SECOFI previously was bound by no time limit to register auto parts manufacturers; today, SECOFI must complete its procedure within ten working days, and the manufacturer is no longer required to supply nonessential information for registry.

For this streamlining we must thank the November 1995 establishment of the Economic Deregulation Council, as well as congressional reform bills that reduce the length of judicial procedures in civil and mercantile cases. The net effect of these reforms is to reduce business costs and minimize potential bribe scenarios.

Tariffs and Duties for Businesses

A plethora of international and bilateral trade agreements (NAFTA, GATT) has greatly simplified import-export procedures and reduced or nullified tariffs altogether. Besides NAFTA (with Canada and the U.S.) Mexico has established "favored-nation" treaties with Australia, the European Union, Japan, New Zealand, Norway, Switzerland, and a number of third world nations.

Such radical reforms catalyzed rapid results on the business scoreboard. In 1993, Mexico's share of U.S. textile imports was 4.4 percent. By 1996 it had increased to 9.4 percent. The social benefits of NAFTA for Mexico are subject to much polemics (a topic best left for economists and social thinkers), as detractors claim that export figures to the United States often reflect exports from U.S. companies based in Mexico. For this reason I cite the textile industry, which remains populated by Mexican entrepreneurs.

In a visit to Mexican textile operations in Aguascalientes, I shared time with progressive Mexican industrialists who were quite sensitive to employee working conditions and the environment in general. Nowhere in Aguascalientes did I witness any of the documented horror stories typical at *maquiladora* worksites along the northern border. The work atmosphere seemed quite positive, clean, even colorful, in striking contrast to the sweat shops I had once investigated in Los Angeles, California.

TAXES

The once complicated Mexican tax system, a motivation for tax dodging, has undergone a comprehensive overhaul. Bancomext claims that Mexico's business taxes are now lower than those of the U.S.A, Canada, the United Kingdom, Germany, and Japan, and are now less than or competitive with taxes in many developing nations.

Space only allows for a brief summary of Mexican taxes, but ample explanation is available from the business contacts in our Strategic Directory.

Federal Taxes

- Taxes on income, including a minimum tax based on corporate assets
- Value-added tax
- Import duties and export taxes (much less than what they used to be)
- Social security, mandatory retirement savings system and National Workers' Housing Fund contributions.

A few federal excise taxes exist on the usual items (alcoholic beverages, cigarettes, gasoline, telephone service, automobiles, etc.)

Local Taxes

- Property taxes
- Payroll taxes
- Real estate transfer taxes.

The good news is that tax treaties have been signed with Mexico's major trading partners to eliminate double taxation. These partner nations include Belgium, Canada, Denmark, Ecuador, Finland, Germany, India, Italy, Japan, The Netherlands, Norway, Romania, Singapore, South Korea, Spain, Sweden, Switzerland, United Kingdom, and the United States. Negotiated treaties with other countries are likely in the future, so check with the nearest Mexican authority in your area.

Currency

The Mexican peso is a floating currency, and Mexico's Central Bank is no longer permitted to intervene in the market. Devaluations approximately every six years have had scary repercussions, but the apparent stability (at this writing) and the liberalized trade policies may have a long-term effect of stabilizing the currency. One Mexican diplomat, also an historian, confided off the record that the pessimists who predicted a new demise of the Mexican peso have been proven dead wrong. He projects greater economic stability as a direct consequence of Mexico's profound democratic transformation of July 6, 1997.

Just in case, though, your enterprise may hold its bank accounts in dollars, subject to minimum balance requirements, thereby neutralizing the effects of a devaluation.

Indeed, you may be able to do business with a bank from your own country; banks from the United States, Japan, Germany, The Netherlands, France, and Spain now operate in Mexico.

Tariffs and Duties

Tariffs have declined significantly; the highest permissible tariff for importation is now 20 percent, with the average tariff at 11.3 percent. By the time the ink dries on this book, duties for 97 percent of all commerce will have been eliminated.

Labor

Traditionally, Mexico's labor confederation was linked to the dominant PRI party. This corporatist structure prevented the types of strikes that would occur more regularly in other Latin American countries. Salaries are low relative to the cost of living. Somewhere in the near future, employers will face a choice: voluntary salary hikes or labor unrest.

Mexico's labor force has won a number of prestigious international awards for productivity and quality, from companies like Ford, Chrysler and G.M. U.S. and Canadian auto workers, however, were not at all pleased about being displaced as these companies transferred plants to Mexico. In contrast with the European community, NAFTA's free flow of capital between its three member nations is not accompanied by free flow of labor.

Profit-sharing is required by law, and employees are entitled to a percentage of profits determined by the National Profit-Sharing Commission. In the cultural realm, workers must receive a year-end Christmas bonus called *aguinaldo* (at least 15 days salary).

Employers are required by law to enrol in the Social Security Institute, thus providing health benefits (full medical care, medicine, etc.) and social services (daycare centers, three month's paid maternity leave, old-age pensions and death benefits). There is a standard eight-hour work week, with one day compulsory paid rest. Vacations are short by European standards, beginning with six days annual paid vacation and increasing with years of service. These laws on the books are not always followed by employers, but foreign entrepreneurs should view these laws as vital for their rapport with workers.

The liberal benefits policy is counterbalanced by a relatively low scale of wages, which vary greatly from region to region. According to Bancomext's *Industrial Costs in Mexico* (Nov '96), per-hour minimum wages in Ciudad Juárez, right across the border from El Paso, were only $1.15 for skilled labor and a meagre 73 cents for

137

unskilled labor, while across in Texas, the minimum was above $5. Minimum wages in Mexico City were even lower.

In Mexico City, the minimum/maximum monthly salary for an executive plant manager was $3,946/$5,263, while the minimum/maximum for a monolingual receptionist was $105/$211. How do unskilled and semiskilled workers survive on such paltry salaries? From my visits to the homes of such employees, I learned that the preferred survival technique is shared housing. Several working members of the same family live under the same roof, often in cramped quarters.

Most observers agree that measures privatizing and deregulating commerce have reduced the plague of state corruption and unchained the productive process. However, to what extent should such measures be carried forth? The Bancomer financial group declared that Article 123 of the Constitution should be reformed, claiming that job creation is constrained by this pro-labor regulation. The Bancomer study mentions that 30 percent of an employee's salary is now directed to social benefits.

Some sectors of the business community also feel hampered by the new tax code. The president of Comev (the Mexican Confederation of Sales and Market Research) complained that business tax reforms were "so complicated that no one understands them and, on the other hand, they sink businesses, mainly small and medium enterprises, in a sea of bureaucracy."

As business continues to push for fewer regulations, some environmentalists have called for a new law to restore ecological equilibrium. One study showed environmental irregularities in 575 industries in Mexico City alone. Enforcement of environmental provisions in NAFTA is largely voluntary and lacks teeth.

With a paucity of government enforcement of existing environmental provisions, some environmentalists attempt to convince entrepreneurial associations that it is in their own self-interest to clean up the mess and maintain sustainable operations.

These are some of the polemics that surround today's business scene in Mexico.

For more information on setting up a business in Mexico, contact the business organizations listed in the strategic directory and visit the Mexican Embassy in your home country. Stay tuned in the next chapter for one Japanese pioneer's most extraordinary Mexican business adventure.

– Chapter Five –

MEXICAN ADVENTURES

As promised in the introduction, anecdotes with implicit messages on the less tangible aspects the culture are more apt to shed insight on the Mexican character than broad generalizations. Share now the following adventures, both positive and negative, and come to your own conclusions.

GETTING RAILROADED

When Mexican writer Juan José Arreola visited California, I was his guide for the day. I asked the great lyrical satirist many questions, but the one question I should have asked seemed inappropriate at the time.

One of Arreola's classic tales, "El Guardagujas" (The Switchman), narrates the tribulations of a foreign traveler in a country that is probably Mexico. The traveler arrives at a government operated railroad station to purchase a ticket.

When his train does not arrive, he is told by the switchman that schedules are not precise. The switchman even suggests to the traveler that he would be fortunate to get on any train that arrives, even if it were traveling to a different destination.

In one passage the switchman explains to the frustrated passenger that when a bridge is swept away, the passengers must descend from the train and build a new one.

The adjective Kafkaesque is overused by literary critics, but in this case it applies. Was Arreola satirizing Mexican railways, state enterprise, the bureaucracy in general, or the unpredictability of life in Mexico?

The answer is probably all of the above. That was the question I should have asked. But Arreola was so spontaneously eloquent in our conversation that I dared not spoil the afternoon with technical or literary questions.

A year later, I had the chance to test Arreola's story experientially. I would take a train from Mexico City to Mexicali, on the California border. Remembering the nightmarish "El Guardagujas," I took major precautions. I arrived early to the station and assured that my ticket was a first-class reserved seat.

From Mexico City to Guadalajara, the trip was comfortably uneventful and the switchman's ominous imagery faded from my mind.

I would change trains in Guadalajara. I assumed that the throng in the station would be distributed among various trains departing to distinct regions of Mexico.

When it came time to load, however, everyone converged on the same train – my train! My reserved ticket still got me a seat, but it was not pleasant sitting down comfortably when women were carrying children in the aisles and old men, probably veterans from the Cristero wars, were leaning uncomfortably against our seats.

The route from Guadalajara to Mexicali would descend more than 1,500 meters, then skirt the Pacific coast before moving inland in the Sonora desert to sunbaked places like Ciudad Obregón and Hermosillo. I hoped the August rainy season would minimize the tropical heat on the descent to Tepic.

141

As the train hurtled from station to station, more passengers got on. After one winding descent, the vegetation metamorphosed into a psychedelic green. One must pay a steamy price for witnessing such tropical luminosity. Somewhere near Tepic, the train thumped and screeched to a halt. Within minutes the wagon heated up beyond the limits of human suffering.

No one announced the reason for the stoppage, no different than what happens when Amtrak's "City of New Orleans" stops inexplicably on the Great Plains somewhere between New Orleans and Chicago. The usual cause of such a stoppage is a slow freight train approaching in the other direction. Perhaps the tracks turn into a single pair and the freight train climbing from the coast needs to pass at this point where there is a two-way bed of tracks.

The encroaching humidity thickened to the point where campesino machetes could slice it. Perhaps the passengers from the first wagon had descended to rebuild a washed-out bridge.

One ascertains cultural traits by observing group dynamics under distressing circumstances. As the train lay inert, seated passengers got up and offered their privileged places to those who were tilting and wilting in the aisle. I followed the same procedure.

It was not simply a question of offering seats to senior citizens, pregnant women, and children. Anyone in the aisle seemed to be granted the right to sit down, and that meant women and children rising to offer their seats to healthy males.

I feared that the initial civility might break down at night, when passengers would be desperate for a precious piece of sleeping space. I recalled sadistic experiments in which rats were placed in over-crowded environments and turned into cannibals.

A freight train thacked by in the other direction and my hopes were lifted to new heights. Our train would start, fresh air would come through the open windows, and with cold drinks and tamales from vendors at the next station, the worst would be over.

But the train did not start up, and the freight train theory was suddenly dubious. Arreola's switchman would have warned me to not be so naive. He would question me as to why I needed to find a logical explanation for every event.

A half hour later, another freight train passed, and another ten minutes later, our train jolted to a start. But the air coming in through the open windows was too thick with humidity to cool down the wagon, which now resembled an overcrowded prison censured by human rights advocates.

At Tepic, food and drink was available from platform vendors: once more, a trace of optimism. Night would bring fresh air, and perhaps some of the passengers, now about four per available seat, would descend at Tuxpan, Tecuala, and Mazatlán.

Neither scenario materialized. More people got on and tropical rains only added to the humidity. The game of musical chairs proceeded, to the music of the thumping rails. A pregnant woman offered me her seat.

"No, that wouldn't be fair," I said.

"I'll get plenty of rest later," she said. "Please sit down for a while. I'll tell you as soon as I need to sit."

I slumped in the seat, saving energy for the tribulations of a sleepless night. An elderly woman from the seat in front of me got up and offered her place to the pregnant woman.

Next to me was Rodolfo, a tailor who lived in Tijuana. We had a few things in common, as he too was a horse-player. We planned to get together in the near future, should we survive the trip, to play the horses at Caliente, which at that time was still running live racing. (Australians know Caliente as the site of the heroic winning streak of their champion Phar Lap.)

At night, mats were placed on the floor of the aisle for the children and the elderly. I had surrendered my seat. A tropical deluge allowed for me to take off my shirt and shower in the space between cars. One does not usually remember trivial events like showers, but I will never forget the caress of the tropical rain on the back of my neck and down my back.

There would be one more dark, deep night before the end of this pilgrimage. During the long hours, everyone in our particular wagon got to know everyone else, as the musical chairs arrangement allowed for new sets of companions each time it was one's turn to sit down.

I wondered whether there was any leadership behind the democratic seat-sharing system, or whether such a thing as spontaneous democracy can exist. I recalled some lines from an essay of Carlos Fuentes, written after a devaluation, in which he wrote of the resiliency of Mexicans to find makeshift solutions under extremely adverse circumstances.

Rodolfo and I had a few more opportunities to converse, and we planned a strategy for pooling our resources in the Pick 6, a bet created by Caliente to attract gamblers from across the border. It was nice to dream of a fertile betting coup as we now crossed the parched Sonoran desert.

Somewhere between Ciudad Obregón and Hermosillo, Lupita, who had been sitting with me and sharing her yearnings, would be descending to a conservative small-town life after having been tantalized by the big city. Her boyfriend would be waiting for her. But her recently-acquired dreams for studying and becoming a professional would sound foreign to her fiance, who could not imagine why she would not be perfectly happy settling down on his small cattle ranch.

The train stopped at her town and Lupita got off. Her boyfriend was waiting there. They kissed, he thinking about the wonderful years they would spend building the ranch, and she thinking of returning to Mexico City to become an executive secretary, or maybe even an architect.

I was now back again with Rodolfo. A few weeks after my return to L.A., I would drive down to see him, pick him up at his tailor shop, and arrive at Caliente, where we would attempt to hit six straight winners and share a pot of a hundred thousand dollars. If we could survive this choking-hot Arreola nightmare on rails, why couldn't we continue to challenge the whole notion of chaos. My thoughts returned to Arreola's great story. When the train reached a spot with no bridge, the passengers would collectively build a new one. They would receive no help from government bureaucrats. Their democracy would be spontaneous and without leadership.

Was this humane finale to what could have been a gruesome nightmare somehow related to Mexican cultural patterns? Or was it the result of the unique dynamics within one atypical passenger car?

Visually, the cars in front of and behind our wagon looked the same as ours, more crowded but less dismal than the passenger bus in a Daumier painting. Whichever car one was in, when the need arose to use the bathroom at the end of the wagon, it would be necessary to step through sleeping bodies on the ground with the utmost agility.

What remained after our arrival in Mexicali for Rodolfo and me was a comfortable bus trip to Tijuana through the spectacular heights of La Rumorosa rock formations, as the sun set on a rare adventure in which an intrinsic democratic spirit emerged without the need for a national leader or local *cacique*: the spontaneous creation of humane order out of total chaos.

NATIVE GRINGO INTRODUCED TO MEXICAN CYNICISM

It was too good to believe. A three-month sublet, furnished, with telephone, in a fashionable Ejército Nacional neighborhood of Mexico City, for the price of an unfurnished flat in a slum in Tacuba. From a public phone I dialed the number of the *Excelsior* classified ad. A Licenciado Baez answered the phone.

Licenciado could mean lawyer or simply degreed professional. He tripped over his words in a jittery way, not like a generic, smooth-talking lawyer.

"Ah, so you're a writer," he said. "I'm an attorney but I teach at the National University. I would like an intellectual in my apartment. It's yours if you want it."

We met at the apartment late that afternoon. I was ten minutes early, like a good Gringo, not wanting to lose the opportunity. He was right there in front of the building waiting for me. A slick business suit trimmed his stocky frame. Smooth olive complexion, dark, bushy eyebrows, neatly trimmed black hair, shiny black shoes completed the first impression. Missing was the typical mustache. He was a real specimen. Not a speck of dust on his lapel. Not the slightest wrinkle in his pants.

The second-floor apartment was better than I'd imagined. Danish furniture with fine woodwork and Mexican pink cushions, parquet floors as shiny as Baez's shoes, with colorful indigenous area rugs. I'd have to work to keep the place this clean. A view of the traffic on Ejército Nacional, which streamed by on both sides of a green boulevard with manicured gardening. A small but well-equipped kitchen. Mattresses not overly soft. And most important, a telephone, which I thought I needed to do business.

I later discovered that you can't get too much accomplished over the phone. It's not like in the States, where people prefer doing business by phone rather than in person. In Mexico, most important business decisions should be made in person. But the phone remains a vital tool, especially in Mexico City, where getting from one place to another for direct contact is not an easy task.

Baez asked for only $200 in deposit, along with the first month's rent. He spoke with a permanent jitter, as if he were in a hurry to leave. I would soon find out why he did not wish to hang around.

At 8:00 that evening, the phone rang. I knew it wasn't for me, so I'd take Baez's messages.

"I want to speak to Licenciado Ceniceros," said a mature but brusk male voice. He didn't say *por favor*. None of the obligatory courteous phrases that initiate conversation in Mexico. He said *quiero* (I want) when you should begin with *quisiera* (I'd like) or *me gustaría* (it would please me).

"I'm sorry," I responded. "I just moved here, and I don't know a

Ceniceros. Are you sure you don't wish to speak with a Licenciado Baez?"

"Who are *you*?"

"I told you, I just moved here."

"Look," he said, angrily now, "I know you're covering for Licenciado Ceniceros. I paid him three hundred dollars to solve a problem I have, and he hasn't done a thing. He won't answer my calls."

"Tell you what," I said. "I'll ask Baez, the guy who rented me this place, if he knows Ceniceros."

"Don't try to con me," the voice said. "I know you're covering for him."

"I assure you I know nothing about this. Please leave your number."

The next call came the following morning. The woman had an Argentine accent, pronouncing the LL like a J, with an Italian sing-songiness.

Unlike the first caller, she was not angered when I told her I'd just moved in. She pleaded:

"Licenciado Ceniceros has my passport. He told me he was going to arrange for my Mexican residency. He has my deposit."

I let her know I was thoroughly confused. She believed me and left her number.

The next woman to call, interrupting my cup of coffee, was not so kind. Licenciado Ceniceros had received her TV in lieu of payment; he was supposed to have gotten her son out of jail. Weeks had passed and there was no word from Ceniceros. I was his flunky, she said, and equally to blame.

"People like Ceniceros and you should be in jail, not my son," she snarled.

I asked her for her phone number. She had no phone. She would call me back tomorrow at the same hour.

There was no food in the refrigerator and I was hungry. But my curiosity was stronger than my yearning for eggs with *chorizo* sausage and beans. I would first investigate my landlord.

After a few phone calls to various departments of the Universidad Nacional Autónoma de México (UNAM), I found a friendly voice, a woman named Carmen, who promised to peel through all the UNAM directories to find out in which department Juan Ramón Baez taught classes.

If I went out now for my super-cholesterol breakfast I might miss Carmen's return call and maybe never hear from her again. I waited.

By 11:00, I had given up. Carmen would probably never call. I decided that she had been sent by a Supreme Being to prevent me from clogging up my human plumbing. Feeling vulnerable, I postponed my inevitable encounter with spicy chorizo, purchasing instead two bags of healthy groceries from a nearby supermarket. I prepared *guacamole* salad. Mash a fresh avocado, dice onions, tomatoes, hot chile peppers, and cilantro. The cilantro herb makes the difference. I warmed the corn tortillas on top of the oven, flipping them over two at a time.

As I was about to take my first bite, the phone rang. It was not Carmen. The voice sounded older, and quite distressed. Her name was María Cristina. If Licenciado Ceniceros did not act quickly, within days or hours, she said, she was going to be arrested for having attacked her live-in boyfriend. Who was going to care for the kids when she was locked up? Not that good-for-nothing. Not that Pedro, who was living off her and wouldn't leave the house when she had tried to boot him out.

I ate my gaucamole and washed it down with manzanilla tea, great for digestion at nearly over 7,000 feet above sea level. All the while, I debated whether or not to call Baez and get this thing straightened out.

Outside, dark clouds drifted above like giant blimps, accompanied by a clap of thunder and a burst of spirited rain that lasted less than a half hour but left the street gutters flooded: a typical cleansing mechanism of the summer rainy season.

I dialed Baez's number but there was no answer, of course not. He must have been at the university.

I went downstairs and hopped on a bus to Chapultepec Park for a half hour of jogging. In Mexico City's rainy season from June through August, you can find days when the thick yellow smog is washed away by the rains. You take advantage of those moments, when the air is perfumed with the smell of eucalyptus and outdoor taco stands.

That evening, Baez told me over the phone, in his typical fluttery voice, that he knew nothing of a Licenciado Ceniceros, that it was all a mystery to him.

My second day was a carbon copy of the first: phone calls from desperate people, some enraged, others pleading, all of them fearing that they'd been stiffed by Licenciado Ceniceros. They gave me their phone numbers, not out of trust but because they had nothing to lose.

I considered unplugging the phone, vetoing the plan on the grounds that one revealing call might resolve the mystery. The next call was a surprise. It was from Carmen, who explained that with over a hundred thousand students at UNAM, she had to go through a lot of directories.

"I'm sorry, there is no Juan Ramón Baez in any department of the university," she said. If I'd have known her better, I'd have asked her to check out Ceniceros. But she'd already provided services beyond the call of duty, information digging for a stranger she knew only by telephone.

I confronted Baez that evening.

"Licenciado Baez," I said, "I believe Licenciado Ceniceros is you. There's no other explanation for these crazy calls."

If he had spoken with a twitch in his voice before, this time his syllables climbed and descended like caged hamsters. His voice rose an octave. I imagined him brushing a speck of dust from his tailor-made suit with manicured nails.

"Listen here," he retorted. "I gave you a good deal. Nowhere else would you find such an agreeable rent. If I were you, I wouldn't be so ungracious. I assure you there is some mistake on the part of the phone company."

I was going to confront him on his fictitious teaching job at UNAM but for what purpose? I'd already confirmed he was lying through the teeth. And there was a veiled threat in his "If I were you."

The next day, with a folder full of phone numbers of disgruntled Ceniceros clients, I called the police. After a few incorrect extensions, I was connected with an inspector García.

García sounded ecstatic. He had been looking for more leads for his investigation on Ceniceros. He was truly grateful. I wanted more information about Ceniceros over the phone but he preferred to meet me at my apartment.

I told him about the folder of names. I'd get those people to show up together to meet with him. A Ceniceros-victim support group.

What a turnabout! The same folks who would have gladly lynched me were now viewing me as a savior. The time and date were set: twelve thirty, Wednesday, so that those "clients" fortunate enough to be employed could use their lunch break.

The Meeting: They say that the Mexicans arrive late, that they have no concept of time. For this meeting, everyone arrives on time, fourteen of them. Only one is late: Inspector García. 1:00 pm. García has still not arrived. 1:15. He's still a no-show.

The clients share their stories. If nothing else, the session is therapeutic. It is good for each victim to know he or she is not alone. Mentally, I add up how much Ceniceros has embezzled. An extra three hundred in rent from me would have been a drop in the bucket. In fact, he should have been paying me for the service.

At 1:30, I phone the precinct. After a few secretaries cannot help me, I am connected to Inspector Arriaga.

"I'm quite sorry," he says. "Just yesterday, Inspector García was transferred to San Luis Potosí."

He should have said "banished." No one wants to work in San Luis Potosí. Maybe Puebla or Guadalajara or Acapulco, but not San Luis Potosí, at the edge of the desert.

Suddenly I fear that my visitors might suspect that the whole thing is a ruse. But they respond with solidarity, as if I too am now their accomplice, a fellow victim.

"We should have known," says one older man. "Here in Mexico, if something happens to us and the police are coming, instead of calling them for help, we run away."

And another: "Ceniceros has influence. No doubt he got them to transfer García."

One by one they file out.

A woman who lives on the third floor is coming back up the stairs with her groceries. She asks me what's going on. I have nothing to lose so I tell her the truth.

"Let me offer you some advice," she says. "Stay out of this. Licenciado Ceniceros, he has his private *granaderos* (armed police). You seem like a nice man. Don't get involved."

I consider moving out after my first month. But the rent is good, and the location perfect. Each day I receive fewer phone calls, until they stop altogether. Ceniceros has surely moved his scam to another apartment.

Confrontation with Ceniceros. A few weeks before I am to vacate the apartment, a helpful lady friend trying to defrost the refrigerator hammers too hard on the ice and the refrigerator dies.

That's fine. I can live for three weeks without a refrigerator. But Baez, I mean Ceniceros, has arranged to return my $200 deposit after he inspects the place.

The fateful inspection day arrives and I wonder what will happen when he finds his refrigerator out of order. The nitpicky Baez/Ceniceros will find his parquet floor a little less shiny and the cushions on his Danish furniture a little less bright pink. But that will pass. The problem is the refrigerator. I want my $200.

My lady friend, Rosa, volunteers to be on the scene to distract Ceniceros. She feels responsible, so she brings her sister along to flirt with him.

I instruct the ladies to "call him Baez, not Ceniceros."

Just before he arrives, I buy an ice cold litre of milk, a piece of Oaxaca cheese and a can of Tecate beer. If he opens the door and touches the cold Tecate, he'll know the refrigerator is functioning just fine.

As usual, he is dressed impeccably. I'm nervous. There's a jittery sound in my voice, as if I were the scamster, not Ceniceros. Rosa gives me a nudge in the ribs, as if to say "calm down, there's nothing to it." I'm not so sure, not with the detail-oriented Ceniceros.

The two women chat with him. His distracted inspection begins superficially. He enters the kitchen, inspects the curtains, caressing the lace.

He doesn't even open the refrigerator. After going through the other rooms, chatting all the while with Rosa and her friend, he opens his billfold.

He hands me some crisp bills that are so new they stick together when I try to count them.

"Don't worry," he chides. "It is all there. I trust you. You should trust me."

He can now reoccupy an apartment that will no longer be receiving angry phone calls, and begin anew.

Mexicans are often accused of beings cynics. They don't trust the police, they don't trust the politicians, and they don't believe what they see on the TV news. They think we Gringos are naive.

I once had a folder with 23 names, 23 people who trusted Licenciado Ceniceros. That makes 22 more Mexicans who are now cynics, and one Argentine lady who is grateful to be home in Buenos Aires.

A NORTH-SOUTH ROMANCE

One great truth about Mexico is that cynicism, as we've seen in the Ceniceros incident, can coexist with its opposite, romanticism, as seen in the saga of El Superbarrios. In some Western cultures, we must choose what is right and valid from two opposite phenomena. But in Mexico cynicism and romanticism are simultaneous and sometimes overlapping realities.

We've just finished a story that will turn romantics into cynics. It is thus appropriate to relate another story that may convert the most fervent cynic into a romantic.

Back in 1961, Andrew and Sandra Sonner made their first trip to Mexico. They were young and childless. This began a romance between three parties: Andy, Sandy and Mexico. On a stringent budget, they lived with a Mexican family and attended the National University of Mexico.

On the way back to the United States, via bus and train, they happened to stop off at the colonial town of San Miguel Allende. It was a period when Kerouac beatniks would roam the cobblestone streets by day and drink tequila by night. San Miguel Allende was an outdoor art museum, with its pastel facades, wrought-iron window grilles, and wood-sculpted colonial doors. The Sonners were hooked.

Over the past 35 years, they have returned to Mexico, to a variety of places, for a variety of reasons: a drive to Guanajuato in 1974, a flight to Yucatán in 1978. By then, they had six children, and all of them experienced the land of the Mayan civilization.

A most memorable voyage for the Sonners was a third-class bus trip down the Baja California peninsula to La Paz, an overnight ordeal that would have made cynics out of those less romantically attached to Mexico. The bus trip was followed by a ferry ride to the coastal city of Mazatlán, and then a spectacular train ride through the Copper Canyon (Barranca del Cobre) to Chihuahua, through 86 tunnels, across 39 bridges, with a seat for every passenger.

Andrew has been a top cop, a County Attorney, while Sandra has directed a continuing education program at a Maryland community college. It could be argued that their travels in Mexico have enhanced their understanding of people who are different and thus enriched their careers. Andrew Sonner has been a truly enlightened and humanistic law enforcement official, instrumental in creating alternative sentencing programs for nonviolent offenders. Sandra has managed a challenging and eclectic program of classes, including unique subjects that other less adventurous programs would shy away from.

Here's an hypothesis admittedly too intangible to prove. After having worked with, interviewed, or taught hundreds of people who have done serious travel in Mexico, I suspect that the inherent creativity and humanism in Mexican life, as well as the country's distressing social contradictions, broaden and deepen the perspectives of one's social and professional life.

As parents, Sandy and Andy must concur, for they have allowed their two daughters, when in their teens, to each spend six-week periods living with Mexican families, one in Guanajuato, and the other in both Coyoacán and Cuernavaca. How many parents would encourage teenage daughters to go off to a strange land on their own?

"I have always told my family," Sandy says: "if I ever run away, it will be to Mexico."

The Sonner family romance with Mexico has now extended to a third generation. In 1997, Andy and Sandy went to Puebla to attend a wedding and took with them their young grandson Andy. In 1995, they had recreated some of their family memories by taking an entourage of 15 for an adventurous trip to Puebla, Oaxaca and the Pacific port of Puerto Escondido.

What does Sandy find so attractive about Mexico? "We have never been disappointed," she says, "in finding friendliness, color, warmth, history, sociology."

TEPOZTLÁN: THE GOLF WAR

Survey of Spanish students: what has been the single greatest impact of your travels and studies in Mexico? The most frequent response was "an increased social awareness." The events in Chiapas between 1994 to the present may overshadow other lessons of living history in Mexico, but from Tijuana to Tapachula, Mexico continues to produce real-life sociology workshops that no text book can equal. One of these fascinating lessons took place in 1996 in Tepozlán.

Tepoztlán, Morelos, population about 13,000, at an eternal spring altitude of 1,701 meters, is only 80 kilometers south of Mexico City and attracts weekend refugees from the smoggy metropolis.

The idyllic setting lured multinational corporate development interests to build a golf course and resort in this radiant green valley surrounded by sculpted cliffs. Topoztlán is also the alleged birthplace of Quetzalcoatl, the pre-Hispanic social reformer. The Aztecs had awaited the return of Quetzalcoatl to save them from their cruel Gods.

Tepoztlán's Indian traditions have attracted an array of new-agers, artists, writers, and environmentalists.

The golf course/resort would be the issue that unleashed a culture clash between opposite world views. They called it "The Golf War," an ecological rebellion against the water-guzzling golf course. Members of the town council who had been seduced by the developers were locked out by the ecological-indigenous coalition. The new local government called itself the "Free Autonomous Municipality of Tepoztlán" in the "Cuauhnahuac Bioregion."

A series of militant demonstrations culminated in the wounding and killing of several townspeople. The proven threat of death failed to discourage the townspeople, local ecologists, and neighboring farmers, who ultimately defeated the developers. The victors reaffirmed the ecological basis of their triumph, referring to unreasonable water requirements for the proposed developments, threats to agricultural use of land, and the potential loss of the traditional lifestyle of the local people.

With this recent bioregional history, Tepoztlán was the ideal site for the Seventh Turtle Island Bioregional Gathering, and bioregionalists were invited by the town host, the Earth Guardian Vision Councils. The "Consejo de Visiones" is a broad-based organization including environmental activists, Aztec religion revivalists ("conchero" dancers), new-age rainbow family people who live ecological lifestyles,

155

back-to-landers, and bioregionalists, those who oppose the global economy with what they consider a more humane way of life based on local cultures and defined by the regional watersheds: "a holistic view of the place as the primary basis for bringing about beneficial changes."

"The transient industrial, globalist segment of society," explains Peter Berg, a San Francisco-based bioregional leader attending the Tepoztlán gathering, "controls the modern context to such a large degree that bioregionalism is suddenly being clung to as a kind of life raft.

"In Tepoztlán," adds Berg, director of the Planet Drum Foundation, "the people on the City Council come from old time, peasant-based Indian families. They are not modern industrialist, globalist, or middle class people."

Also participating in the November 1996 gathering was a *curandera* (natural healer), a gypsy performing group, and political representa-

Photo: Doug Aberley

"Can't be sold. No to the golf course!" *Reminder of the golf war on a Tepoztlán wall.*

tives of the Zapatistas (returned to the state of the original Zapata rebellion for land and liberty). In a show of solidarity, local farmers supplied food to the gathering.

The *curandera* opened the event by holding a goblet fuming with large chunks of incense. An incantation included a request for a beam of light of truth and understanding from the center of the universe. With her two male assistants, describes Berg, "she approached each person in the assembly, moved the goblet up and down in front of their bodies, and intoned thanks to Tonantzín, Aztec deity of the earth … her attendants dipped large bouquets of branches into pails of water and whipped bursts of spray into the air above the crowd to conclude the ceremony."

Peter Berg concluded that "northerners" like himself "experienced the wealth of human and cultural values that abounds in the Spanish-speaking Americas in a direct way undistorted by economic and social lenses."

Tepoztlán is a small town, yet this was the largest planned gathering in the history of the bioregional movement. Only 80 kilometers from the most enormous and polluted city in the world, Tepoztlán asks us to seek answers to Mexico's economic problems on a small human scale.

ONE FAMILY'S DILEMMA: LIFELONG SECURITY IN JAPAN OR UNKNOWN HORIZONS IN MEXICO?

The opposite of one great truth may be another great truth. The bioregional approach of Tepoztlán seems both romantic and practical. It makes lots of sense.

Yet, the opposite internationalist approach of *Compañía Cosmo* appears to be equally valid. The adventure of Mr. Kozo Nakahara, a truly international entrepreneur, may serve as a model for how to cross the great cultural bridge that leads to Mexico.

Nakahara was born in 1931, during the rise of Japanese imperialism. "My generation was a complete tragedy," he says. "For example, two of my high school teachers died in the street."

As a malnourished teenager, Nakahara recalls envying the occupying U.S. soldiers, some of whom were Puerto Ricans and Mexican Americans.

A minor incident or short phrase, insignificant at the moment, may spark a major transformation in one's life. A friend of Nakahara recommended that he study Spanish as well as English. Through his Spanish study, he became interested in Latin America, and studied Latin American economies in college.

He recalls seeing Mexican movies, Buñuel's *Los Olvidados* and *La Perla* starring Emilio "El Indio" Fernández. Both films expressed brutal realities of Mexico; Nakahara was attracted to Mexico by more than simple exoticism.

Following graduation, Kozo Nakahara worked for a multinational trading company, Marubeni Corporation, where he learned the export business with stints in Sydney, Cuba, and Mexico.

For twelve years, Nakahara and his family stayed in Mexico. When they were relocated to their native Tokyo, Nakahara feared that he and his wife and children might have problems readapting to Japan. The culture shock of returning to Japan was accompanied by philosophical doubts, as Nakahara had begun to consider the corporation he'd worked for as a good example of "Japanese imperialism."

His two daughters, one of whom had been born in the land of Cuauhtémoc, asked Nakahara: "Dad, why did you bring us to a country that's so difficult to live in?"

Several months later, the Nakaharas viewed a documentary about Mexico, with magueys, mariachis, and Guadalajara. Suddenly, they were all crying.

"Why don't we return to Mexico," Kozo Nakahara asked. They all agreed. Nakahara resigned from the company, renouncing lifetime security, and becoming the target of criticism from his work companions. He should have maintained a lifelong commitment to a company that had treated him generously. Why would he abandon his companions for a far-off land?

With $5,000 compensation and without greater resources, the Nakaharas returned to Mexico, and Kozo Nakahara worked on a commission basis until he could save enough money to found Cosmo in 1981, in association with three Mexican investors. Compañía Cosmo would export Mexican fruit to Japan.

Traditionally, Mexican producers waited for foreign buyers to come to them. Cosmo would go to the buyers. Nakahara would operate on two principles.

"First you have the encounter between two different cultures and idiosyncrasies, whose customs and tastes are different. Producers must go abroad themselves, carrying samples, and getting to know the differences in culture, tastes and idiosyncrasies."

A second principle is to introduce products directly without triangulation. "Japanese consumers think that Mexican avocados that are sold in Japan are actually from the United States." Cosmo policy has been to dignify Mexican products, which had suffered by having been exported through intermediaries who hid the true origin of the products.

Nakahara believes that profound connections should be created between the two countries doing business.

"When all is said and done, we work with human beings and not with numbers nor with papers." What is needed is "a true adaptation of the product to the needs of the country in question"

Nakahara says that the Japanese market is one of the most difficult in the world.

"For them, it is more important how the fruit looks than even the flavor." He is referring to the culinary art of *kaiseki*, which emphasizes the presentation of the food.

Cosmo works with local Mexican farmers, offering technical assistance so that they can produce the type of fruit that is accepted in the receiving country. Bioregionalists might cringe, but the types of fruits exported by Cosmo had a limited regional market in the first place, and would simply rot on the tree.

Cosmo maintains excellent relations with producers, who are paid in full within 15 days of receipt of product. Producers are assisted in every step along the way, from financing to cover the cost of seeds, to technological advice, to packing.

Nakahara is proud to send two or three employees each year from Mexico to Japan or to other importing countries, to learn the cultural idiosyncrasies and meet personally with clients. Employees are also given courses in the theory and practice of international commerce. Instructors are often employees from within the company, although outside experts are brought in as well.

These practices have paid off, not only in earnings for the company and its employees and producers, but with a prestigious 1996 National Exporter's Award for best trading company, presented to Mr. Nakahara directly by President Ernesto Zedillo.

After my own experience living on a ranch in the beautiful state of Michoacán, I feel personally vindicated by the achievements of Compañía Cosmo, some of whose producers come from Michoacán. I would wake up at sunrise and go walking into the orchards, stepping unintentionally on rotting fruit. Thousands of sweet *guayabas* and other non-traditional and traditional fruits, untouched by the human hand, were returning to the earth they came from.

"Why can't you sell the fruit?" I asked José, the owner.

"Here in Mexico, the amount we'd get for the fruit won't even pay for the transport, and foreign markets are closed to us."

That was before Compañía Cosmo came along. Now, fruits like the tuna (cactus pear), Persian lime, pitahaya (dragon fruit), carambola (star fruit), chirimoya, and the very same guayaba (fruits that would grow naturally far in excess of the demand from the national market) are being exported successfully by Cosmo, which also exports Mexican vegetables.

Kozo Nakahara considers the export business profoundly linked to a common ground between very distinct cultures. The land of Cuauhtémoc worked its magic on Mr. and Mrs. Nakahara and their two daughters, who themselves became Mexican imports, willing to take a chance on leaving a life of security in Japan to become pioneers in their adopted country.

The Nakahara family is proudly multicultural and most publications from Compañía Cosmo are either bilingual or trilingual (Spanish, Japanese and English).

Kozo Nakahara on the export business: "We work with human beings and not with numbers, nor with papers. What is needed is a true adaptation of the product to the needs of the country in question."

The Nakaharas feel comfortable in their adopted land but what keeps them here is the unknown rather than the familiar.

"Living in a country with a mixture of western and indigenous," writes Mr. Nakahara, "gives me always the sensation and need for a more profound understanding, and perhaps this is what attracts me to continue living in this country."

Nakahara admits that after 40 years in Mexico, he still faces cultural obstacles, especially when deciphering language related to the Catholic religion, which remains foreign to him. On the other hand, his personality has undergone changes directly related to his adopted culture.

Beneath his venerable demeanor, he has a warm sense of humor, which he admits he learned in Mexico.

"I've told my Mexican friends that Compañía Cosmo is small but hot, like the Mexican chili pepper."

Having lived in many countries, he has learned to "despise the arrogance of social and family position that exists generally throughout the world."

From living and doing business in a poor country, Nakahara remains optimistic about the balance between powerful and weaker nations. "As human history shows us, I consider that no people can enjoy prosperity or dominance indefinitely."

With such a philosophy, it is no surprise that Nakahara refuses to hide the keys to the success of his own company. He shares knowledge with potential business rivals in numerous conferences and seminars with exporters in Mexico and Guatemala.

Chapter Six

MEXICO IN CRISIS

... *STRANGER THAN FICTION*

Corruption, intrigue and murder in high places has been so endemic and melodramatic in current Mexican affairs that the great novelist Carlos Fuentes finds fictional portrayal of life at the top to be overshadowed by inconceivable reality. Fuentes now resorts to the genre of journalistic essay, probing beyond newspaper conventions in order to uncover the human drama.

An 85-year-old woman from Guerrero writes poetry about the destiny of her sons, something like "My four sons" or "The Brothers Ruiz Massieu."

One of her two eldest sons is accused of getting a woman pregnant. The girl's irate father, in order to consummate his vengeance, takes no chances and kills both of the lady's eldest sons. Two sons gone.

Two decades later, a third son, the dapper secretary-general of Mexico's ruling PRI leaves a breakfast meeting in downtown Mexico

City and is gunned down. An accused culprit, a PRI congressman, disappears forever.

But a shadowy businessman is indicted. He is Raúl Salinas, brother of former president Carlos Salinas de Gotari. Raúl Salinas is also the former brother-in-law of the murdered man, who was once married to the sister of the president.

Of the original four, one son remains. As deputy district attorney, he is named to investigate the murder of his brother. He accuses the PRI bosses of obstructing his investigation and leaves office, departing with smuggled currency on his way to Europe. But he is detained in Newark Airport, New Jersey, accused of having deposited US$9 million of illicitly-obtained money in U.S. banks within the past ten months.

After being indicted in the U.S., this fourth son is accused of covering up the investigation of the murder of his brother.

Many bizarre subplots to this "Mexican melodrama" complicate the panorama for the visitor to Mexico. An opposition candidate's campaign chairman is murdered. A Catholic cardinal is shot dead at the Guadalajara airport, mistaken for a drug lord, because both cardinal and drug lord had identical automobiles. The PRI candidate expected to succeed Salinas de Gortari is murdered in Tijuana, with public opinion unanimously believing the murder was orchestrated from within the PRI. Mexico's human rights commission confirms that the 1995 killing of 17 peasants involved summary executions and that there was a cover-up by state officials over the incident; Guerrero's governor is eventually forced to resign.

Current president Ernesto Zedillo hires an opposition PAN official with a reputation for honesty as District Attorney, but Antonio Lozano Gracia is later forced to resign in disgrace for not knowing things he should have known about investigations of higher-ups. Zedillo then hires the incorruptible General Gutiérrez Rebollo to head the struggle against drugs; Gutiérrez Rebollo is later fired after revelations of his connections to a drug cartel. The Clinton administration then "certifies" Mexico as having fulfilled its commitments in the war against drug smuggling.

Carlos Fuentes concludes that "reality is stranger than fiction and literature cannot aspire to beat history." At least not Mexican history.

The imposition of neoliberal economics, involving the withdrawal of the State from the economy, was intended to reduce corruption in high places, but the above rash of unbelievably unscrupulous actions suggest that the opposite is occurring. Some Mexicans affirm that nothing has changed with respect to the behavior of the powerful.

However, traditional impunity and cover-ups of political crimes are no longer possible. Officials who in the past would have kept their jobs are today being fired or forced to resign. A more democratic Mexico will never return to the days of the *caudillo* (the populist political boss).

Where does the visitor to Mexico fit in this context? First, it is important to note that Mexico has no monopoly on corruption. Similar melodramas are acted out in most countries around the world. In my country, the United States, four senators of great prestige were implicated in a scandal involving the savings and loan industry. In return for campaign donations, they had failed to investigate shady business practices, and the result was a multi-billion dollar bailout financed by U.S. taxpayers. None of these senators went to jail. Defense industry bribery, Iran-Contra, and campaign finance irregularities are but a few of the recent scandals to affect a country where corruption is supposed to be foreign to its traditions.

This is not intended to mitigate the seriousness of corruption in Mexico. The fundamental question is: are people inherently corrupt, are cultures corrupt, or do corrupt systems ultimately overwhelm good people? Mexican essayist Jorge Castañeda suggests that Mexican corruption is systematic rather than cultural.

"Can one remain honest - that is to say neither corrupt nor an accomplice to corruption - in a system that is rotten from within?" asks Castañeda.

Castañeda illustrates examples of well-intentioned, honest people who are devoured by the system. One of his examples should be of great interest to readers who expect to live, study or do business in Mexico, for it concerns a foreigner. He is a U.S. official of great stature who naively believed that the problem of Mexico was bad people and not bad institutions and that it would be possible for good people to succeed within the same system.

This philosophical perspective caused General Barry McCaffrey, U.S. Drug Czar, to trust that good people, in particular General Rebollo, could clean up Mexico's drug problem without the need to change the institutions around them.

"McCaffrey ended up like a perfect imbecile before his countrymen and his president," writes Castañeda, because he had believed that Mexico's problem was its people and not its institutions.

Castañeda then answers his own question: "Today, not even well-intentioned individuals, honorable and with power, can manage against the systematic Mexican vices ... either we change the system or everyone sinks - we all sink - with it."

"The problem is," Castañeda wrote in *Newsweek* (March 3, 1997), "that the Americans ask the wrong question about Mexico: is there no one honest down there? Of course there is. Most Mexican officials are scrupulous. Unfortunately, they work in an outdated system of single-party rule that compels all too many honest men and women to countenance and eventually conspire in corruption."

With the defeat of the PRI in the July 6, 1997 congressional elections, and the victory of opposition candidate Cuauhtémoc Cárdenas as governor of the Federal District, will corruption abate? Cárdenas believes he can contribute to the rooting out of corruption within Mexico City and its surrounding areas within his jurisdiction. The surprising transparency and integrity of the 1997 electoral process resulted from a profound institutional change in the body governing the elections and other institutions. President Zedillo presided over these changes, fully aware that they would lead to the defeat of his party.

Murders in high places, neoliberal economics, free elections: none of these events make an impact on these participants in the street economy, who continue to play on their battered marimba.

But following the election, seasoned political observers in Mexico predicted that one man like Cárdenas, no matter how earnest he may be, can make few dents in a vast institutional network of corruption.

Prior to the historic election, Carlos Fuentes predicted that "there can't be fraud because the electoral system that we have created is perfectly open and trustworthy."

Fuentes' prediction was proven correct. Journalist Jorge Ramos Avalos was surprised by Fuentes' optimism. "The few other times I've spoken to you, you weren't so optimistic about Mexico's civil society."

"Sure," responded Fuentes. "That's because it is developing, because we have fought for it. After all, one cannot deny his own triumphs. Right? The country is changing. If it were another era, I would tell you something else."

167

The Federal Electoral Institute was one successful change. Will other institutional overhauls follow? These are exciting times in Mexico. With no political party in the majority in congress, positive new agreements unheard of in the past may be possible through democratic negotiation. On the other hand, the old system will be pulling out all stops to ensure its perpetuation, attempting at all levels to co-opt the bright-eyed newcomers, and if that doesn't work, resorting to violence as exemplified by the January 1998 massacre in Chiapas.

One discomforting example of how institutions envelop and dominate the individual concerns this writer. On several occasions, I have been in a position where a modest bribe would get something done quickly. I had a choice: don't pay the bribe and wait for months for the institution to take care of my paperwork, Or pay it and get it done then and there.

The prototypical person receiving the bribe (or was it a fee?) is a low-level bureaucrat earning a paltry salary that cannot suffice for his own support no less the support of his family. It was easy for him and for me to rationalize becoming involved in a "minor" incident of corruption when we witnessed more substantial corruption in circles far above us. Indeed, we might be foolish to not get on with it for a few pesos. When president Salinas's brother Raúl was carting off 30 million at a time in illicit windfalls, what harm was an extra "fee" of 30 pesos?

Today, Raúl is behind bars. With greater transparency in the Mexican system and less impunity for those above, it becomes more difficult for common people like us to rationalize acts of corruption.

The visitor who comes to Mexico in this context of crisis and transition will probably be coming from another country where other forms of crisis, crime and corruption exist. But how will Mexico's unique scenario filter down to the visitor? Much depends on whether Mexico can avert yet another economic crisis, and whether the melodrama of crime and intrigue among the country's powerful will subside.

Surely some of the petty crime that may adversely affect the unprepared visitor (see survival skills in the next chapter) results from a type of behavior by example. "If our leaders can commit murder and get away with it, why can't I snatch a purse?" is an unacceptable yet plausible reaction in some sectors of the population. If you travel on the D.F. metro enough, sooner or later you will witness this sector in action.

The visitor will descend upon a situation of two primary countercurrents, cynicism and romanticism. For every Mexican (and foreigner) who finds greater rationalization for participating in some form of corruption, there are hundreds of others whose ideals can no longer be tainted by what Castañeda refers to as the system, and who commit daring acts of human solidarity or who risk their lives for a principle.

In some ways, the Mexico of today is more refreshing than that of three decades ago when the peso was eternally 12.5 to the dollar, Televisa was censoring the news, and the PRI was apparently defending the principles the Mexican Revolution. Now that everyone knows the truth, Mexico can never return to the good old days. Curiously, the decay of Mexico's ruling elite is accompanied by a cultural renaissance in literature, art, music, film, and journalism.

"The weakening of structures of state control," says anthropologist Maya Lorena Pérez Ruiz, "may contribute to this cultural opening. The State had been accustomed to exercising much control over artistic production."

Will the romantics or the cynics be proven correct in their predictions for the future of Mexico? Off the record, in the aftermath of the July 6 elections, one high-level Mexican diplomat confided with me that he was ecstatic with the irreversible defeat of the corrupt ruling party and could not wait to return to his country to experience a most exciting period of transition.

Chapter Seven

SURVIVAL SKILLS

Too much planning won't allow for serendipity to precipitate a magic encounter or a memorable thrill. In Mexico, the best strategy is to give chance a chance.

In the English language thesaurus there is no opposite for serendipity. Mexico could invent the word "malfortuity," it is a land where anything can happen, both bad and good. For this reason, underplanning could have just as serious consequences as overplanning.

What follows is an annotated list of survival skills that in their totality comprise a method for planning your stay in Mexico but still leave enough open doors for serendipity to step in. Categories are listed in rough chronological order of a typical voyage to this wondrous and contradictory land.

SPANISH LANGUAGE

Mexicans and most other Latin Americans appreciate attempts by visitors to speak Spanish. The Spanish language itself encourages the shedding of linguistic inhibitions, even for those who have a block against language learning. Spanish, unlike English, is basically a phonetic language, with each letter consistently sounding like its name. The English language suggests that there is chaos in the universe and that the Supreme Being has faltered. Well-ordered Spanish cries out "There is a God! and he's an efficiency expert."

An awareness of such clean-cut phonetics coupled with a very basic foundation of vocabulary and grammar can get you through the day. Since a large portion of English shares a Latin root with Spanish, there are numerous "cognates," words that may sound similar or different but have virtually identical spelling and meaning. Only a handful of notable grammatical differences separate English and Spanish.

With more complex or "different" languages, the lag time between the moment of introduction until the moment of practical use is lengthy. With Spanish, the English-speaking student can start speaking from day one.

Phonetics. With most consonants quite similar to English, vowel comprehension plays the strategic role in successful listening. Each of the five vowels never vary in pronunciation.

A is pronounced AH, like the a in father.

E is pronounced EH, like the e in ten or vest.

I is pronounced like a shortened EE like the i in tangerine.

O is pronounced OH, as in for (not quite a "long" o).

U is pronounced like a shortened OO, like the oo in "oops!"

Even before mastering the consonants, these five little vowel sounds allow the learner to say and understand most cognates.

Only two Spanish consonant sounds do not exist in English and might hinder the understanding of cognates: (1) the rr which sounds like a trill (the tongue must flutter) and (2) the j as well as the g (only when it comes before e or i), which sound like a hard h as if one were clearing one's throat. A similar sound exists in Arabic and Hebrew.

There are, however, other consonants that do not sound like their English counterparts:

H is silent.

LL is pronounced similarly to the English y.

Ñ is pronounced like the ni in onion.

R is pronounced like the American double tt in matter.

QU is pronouced like k, with a silent u.

X is the same as its English counterpart, except in words coming from the Nahuatl language, when it sounds like the Spanish j, as in México written Méjico in Spain.

Z is the same as the Spanish and English s as there is no buzzing z sound in Spanish.

A written accent tells the reader that the stress on a word is falling on a syllable other than the normal stressed syllable.

Cognates

Once the phonetics are understood, many hundreds of useful words become immediately accessible. Here are a few cognate groups:

- Virtually all words ending in tion or ssion in English, with occasional minor spelling changes, end in ción or sión in Spanish. Conversación, intuición, nación, comunicación, misión, comisión. Hundreds of other cognates are derived from this group. Example: the verb conversar, to converse, chat.

- Virtually all words ending in ity in English end in idad in Spanish, with only occasional minor spelling changes. Unidad, claridad, entidad. Words derived from the idad group are also cognates. Example: the verb unir, to unite.

- Words from English ending in em or ama (of Greek origin) have their parallels in Spanish with ema and ama endings. Problema, sistema, drama, panorama, tema (theme), etc. Gender: Spanish nouns are masculine (usually ending in o) or feminine (usually ending in a), but this Greek group of words represents an exception, and are masculine. Example: el problema (the problem).

• Hundreds of other frequently used words are derived from the above three groups or are independently parallel to English. The beginner Spanish student starts out with an abundant vocabulary.

Grammar

In Spanish, verbs change their endings (conjugations) according to the subject pronoun. The ending of the verb usually indicates the subject. Even though *yo hablo* means "I speak," the *yo* is not necessary except for emphasis, since the *o* ending indicates first person singular. An excessive use of the *yo* could make you sound egotistical. When conjugating the "you" there is a familiar "tú" and a formal "usted" with different verb endings.

A few other basic differences are:

• Descriptive adjectives follow the noun instead of preceding it (lección *difícil* instead of *difficult* lesson).

• Adjectives agree in gender (male/female) and number (singular/plural) with nouns. Example: *edificio blanco* (white building) is male (*o* ending), and *casas blancas* (white houses) is feminine (*a* ending) and plural (*s* ending).

• One significant difference in perception between the two languages is the verb: to be. Spanish has two verbs that translate "to be": *ser* refers to essence or identity, and *estar* refers to state, condition, or location. "To be or not to be" from *Hamlet* is *ser o no ser*, since it refers to the character's identity. But *cómo está usted*? (How are you?) is derived from *estar* because you're asking the state or condition of the person. Memorize this crucial sentence which will save the day if you have an attack of *turista: Dónde está el baño* (Where is the bathroom?). Notice that we use the verb *estar* because we refer to location rather than essence.

- Another difference in perception is observed in Spanish's two past tenses: the preterit, which views an event as completed, and the imperfect, which describes or re-experiences the past. Preterit: "I went" and imperfect "I was going."

- Object pronouns that accompany verbs go before a conjugated verb, the opposite of English. Example: *te* quiero (I love *you*), another crucial phrase for the romantically inclined.

- Reflexive pronouns *me* (myself), *te* (yourself, familiar), *se* (him/her/yourself), *nos* (ourselves), *se* (themselves) go before conjugated verbs, and the reflexive construction is used much more frequently in Spanish than in English: *Me llamo María* = my name is María (literally: I call myself María); *José se levanta temprano* = José gets up early (literally: José raises himself early). (Note: all English compound verbs with *get* are reflexive in Spanish.)

Other grammatical nuances are of less strategic importance and may be picked up as you learn.

Politeness. For good rapport, use either of two introductory verb conjugations for making requests, both of which mean "I would like" rather than "I want": *quisiera* and *me gustaría* (literally "it would please me").

This summary will help you sift out what is essential when taking recommended non-credit continuing education course in Spanish. Such courses, offered at adult education centers, are more practical and quicker than credit courses at universities, which bog down in abstract details.

Skilled language learners can use the above outline to "wing it" with the help of a pocket dictionary.

Mexicanisms

Most texts illustrate general or universal Spanish. Mexico's Spanish has its unique tonality and vocabulary. The following list introduces frequently-used words or phrases typical of Mexican Spanish. Some

Mexicanisms are derived from the Aztec language, Nahuatl, while others are a product of popular culture. Not included within the list is the custom of shortening words in popular speech. Example: in "Let's get together when we're *tranquilos*," italics means "tranquil" or "at ease", and may be shortened to *tranquis* in urban slang. (General Spanish word in italics/parentheses.)

Aguacate: avocado, (Nahuatl) (*palta*)

Andale/ándele: formal/familiar, means "go to it," "let's go," "hurry up" depending on context

Antojito: a snack food

Atarantado: confused

Bolillo: crusty white bread roll

Bote: jail (slammer); also *tambo, tanque*

Bueno: used to answer the phone, literally: good

Buey: stupid (an insult), literally: ox, pronounced guey

Cacahuates: peanuts (Nahuatl) (*maní*)

Camión: bus, literally: truck (*bus*)

Cantina: bar (*bar*)

Chamaco/a: boy/girl (*muchacho/a*). Also: *chavo, chavalo*

Chamba: gig, job

Chango: monkey (*mono*)

Charro: Mexican cowboy, participant in rodeos

Cheve: beer, short for *cerveza*

Chiches: woman's breasts, vulgar

Chihuahua!: darn it! Also *Caray!*

Chile: hot pepper (Nahuatl)

Chingar: used in numerous vulgar or sometimes popularly acceptable expressions the way *fuck* (English) or *foutre* (French) are used.

Chingadera: something that doesn't work correctly

Chingaquedito: passive-aggressive, literally fucks quietly

Chingón: someone who is abusive or overly aggressive

Choya: head

Choro: gossip

Chulo/a: cute (used in flirting)

Churro: marijuana, literally a fried pastry

Coraje: anger (in other countries, means courage)

Cuate: pal, blood brother; also *carnal* (Mex-Amer)

Ejotes: green beans (Nahuatl)

Elote: corn on the cob (*choclo* in South America)

Esquincle: little brat (Nahuatl)

Fayuca: smuggling of cheap goods like clothes

Feria: change, cash (*cambio*)

Gabacho: someone from the U.S.A. (*gringo*)

Gacho: ugly (*feo*)

Guajalote: turkey (*pavo*)

Guero: white guy (similar to *gringo*)

Hacer berrinches: to have a small tantrum

Huaraches: sandals

Huevón: a lazy man (literally, big-balled)

Jitomate: English word tomato comes from Nahuatl

Lana: money, literally, wool (*dinero, plata*)

le: object pronoun often attached to a command to indicate impatience: *camínale* (walk faster)

Luego luego: right away

Madre: used in many male-to-male insults, the worst of which is *chinga tu madre*, (or just *tu madre!*). A *desmadre* is a total mess-up

Mande: a polite way to ask, what can I do for you?, or simply to acknowledge a request, literally, the imperative: order

Mano: from *hermano*, title for companion (male only)

Marchanta: a street saleswoman

Mero: adj "the very" (*en la mera esquina*=on the very corner); *ya mero* means: ready in a jiffy

Metate: stone bowl/hand tool to grind corn (Nahuatl)

Mordida: bribe (bite)

Mota: marijuana

Órale (pues): let's get it moving (then)

Petate: sleeping mat (Nahuatl)

Platicar: to converse, literally, to preach (charlar)

Padre: equivalent to slang "cool," literally, father

Para servirle: when being introduced, this phrase follows one's name: "María Bernal, to serve you"

Pendejo: insult means "stupid" (literally: pubic hair)

Pelar(se): to split, run off (*se* is reflexive *oneself*)

Regar: to "blow" (sprinkle) "la regaste" (you blew it)

Relajo: wild mischief or confusion

Tantito: a little bit

Tarugo: a clumsy or dumb person

Tener palancas: to be influential (to have pull, leverage)

Tener pegue: to be popular with the opposite sex

Tener pena: to feel ashamed or bashful (to feel sorrow) or: *me da pena* (it makes me bashful)

Torta: sandwich on a *bolillo* roll (cake in So. Am.)

Viejo/a: an endearing term for one's man/woman or father/mother: *mi vieja:* (my old lady); literally, old but a change in tone of voice and *las viejas* means prostitutes

These Mexicanisms open a strategic door to intangible cultural attitudes. A list of Spanish classes for foreigners in Mexico appears in this book's strategic directory.

Communication Skills

The most strategic communication skill is not being afraid to talk. It bears repeating that Latin America peoples welcome attempts by foreigners to speak their language.

On many an occasion, inclusion in or exclusion from a conversation greatly depends on one's knowledge of the theme. The language barrier rises and thickens a few meters when the subject of the conversation is not familiar to the foreigner. By knowing in advance the most popular themes in small talk and conversation in general, the foreigner will increase the probability of comprehending and will have something to offer in exchange.

- **Current events:** Mexico is a very history-conscious country. Discussions on current events (you should read the newspapers) often make historical references. Chapter 1 of this book will provide the historical context. Reading newspapers in Spanish will help you accumulate the vocabulary of current events.
- **Family:** The extended family is still a living tradition in some sectors of Mexican society; vocabulary related to family members is basic to common conversations.
- *Fútbol:* Both men and, to a lesser extent, women may be passionately involved in the progress of Mexico's professional football/ soccer league. Choose a local team and root for it, and you'll be surprised how often you'll be involved in conversation. *Fútbol* is by far the most popular Mexican pastime. There are numerous amateur football leagues for men and women alike. If you play this game, all the better.
- **Farming:** As we have insisted, many urbanized Mexicans may be only a generation removed from their rural past. Knowledge of animal raising and farming will get you involved in many a

conversation. A typical Mexican home has an inner patio with a grand fruit and vegetable garden. This author, a confirmed city boy, was prompted to raise animals and grow fruit and vegetables in a rural homestead after experiencing the connection between the urban and rural of various Mexican friends.

- **Religion:** Mexico is simultaneously a religious and a secular country. When one young woman was accosted by a knife-wielding rapist in an empty-lot short-cut from the bus stop to her neighborhood, she noticed he was wearing a cross. She called his attention to the symbol of the cross he had chosen to wear, asking if a believer in Christ could also be a rapist? The accoster thus backed off and my daughter was saved from a hellish tragedy. Who says that miracles don't exist? What a fitting conclusion to a section on communication skills!

Mexican fans greeting their national soccer team. Football (soccer) is a passion for Mexicans of both sexes. You won't be left out of conversations if you are aware of what is happening in Mexico's professional fútbol league.

179

GETTING THERE

U.S. and Canadian citizens may travel to Mexico with a tourist card, and any proof of citizenship suffices. However, a passport remains the most reliable backup document. Citizens from all other countries need to show a current passport.

Other English-speaking nationalities, including Australia, New Zealand, and the United Kingdom may also receive a tourist card upon presentation of a passport, without the need for a visa. Most other countries require a visa. Citizens of any country should check with the nearest Mexican consulate or international airline flying to Mexico for the most current visa and tourist card requirements.

Caution: if you are traveling to Mexico by land from the United States and are not a U.S. citizen or resident, check U.S. visa requirements ahead of time to assure re-entry into the United States.

Tourist cards may be supplied by Mexican consulates, airlines, or travel agencies, but must be validated upon entry into Mexico by land from the U.S. or Guatemala. The procedure for obtaining a tourist card at the Mexican border office is rather simple. If you wish more than 30 days on your free tourist card, you may request up to 180 days. The reason for your request will determine the number of days you are given by the border official.

It is highly recommended to have one's tourist card in order. But it is very rare that you will ever be asked to show your card.

Tip: when crossing into Mexico by land from a U.S. border city, you may find more than one crossing bridge to choose from. At El Paso, I walked across the truckers' bridge and thus avoided a long line for obtaining my tourist card.

Customs

When entering by land or air, you must pass through customs. At most entry points there is an indoor traffic light. If the light flashes green as you pass (it's rigged to flash green much more often than red), you don't even have to open your suitcases and there is no inspection.

If the light flashes red, your suitcases may be opened and inspected. On a rare occasion, a customs official may question the reason for an electronic gadget, since *fayuqueros* (smugglers) sell such items illegally. Be prepared with a logical explanation for your personal use of such a gadget.

CURRENCY

Border areas and airports have *casas de cambio* (exchange houses), usually kiosks or sidewalk windows. Upon entering the country, you should obtain Mexican pesos as early as possible. Be aware of the exchange rate prior to your entry so that you will obtain the fair market value for your native currency. As these pages are being written, the Mexican peso is on the way up above eight per dollar. But as explained, that rate is subject to minor or major changes, depending on the next devaluation or other economic measures.

HOUSING

For getting involved in the way of life, family-run hotels are much more amenable (and less expensive) than modern chains or theme hotels.

For longer stays, an apartment may be found through the classified ads. There is less privacy in a boarding house (*casa de huéspedes*) but you get to take your meals with interesting people, some locals and other foreign travelers. Shop around and you will find a reasonably-priced room with a private bath.

Another alternative is to live with a family. Most schools offering English or Mexican culture courses to foreigners will have personnel in charge of locating you with a family, but you'll probably have to be registered in a course in order to take advantage of the service.

During different stays in Mexico, I have lived with a family, stayed in *casas de huéspedes*, and rented my own apartment. The choice depends on your persuasion and the purpose of your stay.

TRANSPORTATION

Bus

The most popular way to travel from city to city is by bus. First-class bus service is reliable, comfortable, and not expensive. Second and third-class buses increase the element of chance, and in return for a cheaper fare, your trip will be slower and bumpier.

Many cities have now placed their bus terminal (*Central Camionera* or *Central de Autobuses*) at the outskirts of town. This adds time at both ends of your trip. An urban bus ride from the Central Camionera to downtown may last an eternity. Be prepared to take a taxi if the time factor is crucial. (To avoid an unlikely robbery by a "pirate" taxi driver, take taxis from official taxi stands.)

Train

Train travel is only recommended as an adventure in itself. In most cases, it will be slower than bus travel. The Chihuahua-Pacífico trip through Copper Canyon will inspire a love for railroads.

Air

Air travel within Mexico is relatively inexpensive, with both major airlines, Mexicana and Aeroméxico. If you like eating out, you can eat WAY out by enjoying Mexicana's superb cuisine. A number of newer and smaller airlines with target markets offer great value, good service, plus a safety record that thus far equals the major lines. Shop around.

FOOD

Lovers of Mexican food find it no surprise that a work of literature, the novel *Like Water for Chocolate*, can be structured around Mexican recipes. Mexican food is both extensive in variety and profound in flavor. With virtually every world climate found somewhere in

Mexico, from tropics to snow-covered mountain passes, the diversity of Mexican produce is mind-boggling.

Many products that today are considered universal were born in Mexico, and the proof is in the linguistics. The words *chocolate, tomato,* and *avocado*, come directly from the Nahuatl language and pass on into English, French and other tongues.

The fundamental zest of Mexican food comes from its use of pungent or piquant sauces even in the most proletarian eateries. In Europe, corn is considered appropriate for animals; but in Mexico, the tortilla, a round, flat crepe-like substitute for bread, fashioned from ground corn flour, is not only a food staple but a utensil for scooping up the food and sauce.

No law exists against using the standard fork and knife. But in traditional settings, the tortilla may be employed as a substitute. One breaks it and folds it into a scooping instrument. Both food and "utensil" are thus consumed.

"The art of Mexican street food" is a book waiting to be written. The *taco* is the foundation of Mexican street stands. A tortilla is wrapped around various kinds of meat in sauces, or beans for vegetarians. Herbs such as *cilantro*, and hot sauces added as one pleases, complete the formula.

Other fast-food snacks include: *sopes* (thicker tortillas sprinkled with grated white cheese and onion); *burritos* (not unlike tacos but with flour tortillas and with refried bean spread inside mixed with whatever meat one desires); *tostadas*, toasted tortillas served un-folded, with meat and salad topping; *flautas* (fried tortillas rolled into the shape of a flute with strings of meat inside); *tortas,* a Mexican sandwich in which the crusty *bolillo* bread is sliced in half and grilled inside face down, then filled with refried beans, avocado, tomato, onion, and a choice of carnivore filling, with hot sauce or hot *jalapeño* pepper; *quesadillas* (tortillas with melted cheese); *guacamole*, an avocado salad with tortillas or tortilla chips; *chilis rellenos* (large mildly hot peppers, usually stuffed with cheese and deep fried); and

Public markets offer personal service, fresher food, and lower prices than supermarkets.

of course, *enchiladas*, same as tacos but with melted cheese or chicken inside and a cheese topping, and baked or lightly fried, with a moist sauce on top. These are but a few of Mexico's enormous variety of fast foods.

One may approach this cuisine from two opposite perspectives. On the one hand, Mexico seems to be a carnivorous country. It is not unusual for steak to be served for breakfast. On the other hand, the flavor of Mexican food depends greatly on the chili peppers, herbs, avocado, and above all, the accompanying beans. Remove the chicken, ham, pork or sausage from a *torta* sandwich and you are left with a most complete meal from a nutritional standpoint and a solution for the vegetarian.

I have spent time with Mexican families whose diet is virtually vegetarian but balanced nonetheless. Protein is derived from eggs, a wide variety of cheeses, boiled milk with coffee, and above all beans.

Cilantro, avocado, tomato, onion, garlic, chili peppers, and the tortilla are the staples for a tasty diet.

Choosing a Restaurant

Ever since my favorite Paris bistrot was excluded from the major Paris travel guides, I have decided that recommending specific restaurants is a futile exercise. In choosing a good Mexican restaurant, there are several techniques:

- **Setup:** Make sure food displays are not sitting in the sun.
- **The people test:** Choose a place where many people are eating, thus assuring that food will not be reheated.
- **The sauce test:** Walk by the tables and make sure that the dishes are bathed in sauces. The best Mexican food at all social levels uses exquisite sauces.
- **The authenticity test:** Check the menu for the most authentic foods and/or ones that are most difficult to prepare, such as *mole* (recipe to follow), *pozole* (an indigenous hominy stew), *huachinango* (a red snapper fish plate from Veracruz).
- **Cleanliness test:** Check for cleanliness, but beware of modern facades. Cleanliness does not mean that the place has to be new and expensive. One quick cleanliness test is to check for soap and toilet paper in the bathroom.
- **Chains:** Avoid chains like Denny's and VIPS, whose prices far exceed the quality of their bland food. Hotel food is usually overpriced and less authentic, although I've been pleasantly surprised on occasion.
- **Regional dishes:** Just when you think you've gotten to know Mexican food, a new regional dish materializes. Regional dishes must not be missed. *Espinazo* (pork spine), for example, in a green sauce made from herbs like parsley and *epazote*, chilis and beans originates in Oaxaca but I've found it in Mexico City. If you don't eat meat, rice bathed in the sauce from espinazo is extraordinary.

Photo: Juan Carlos Vega

A Tlaxcala outdoor restaurant: ambience and good food.

- **The best bargain:** The best food bargain, we insist, is the *comida corrida* fixed-price lunch, with several courses including *caldo* (soup), *sopa* (which is not soup but a rice or noodle dish), the main course, with a meat dish usually bathed in sauce along with beans and tortillas, and a simple desert or coffee. Some boarding houses are open to the public and offer home-made food.
- **Market stalls:** Public market stalls present a dilemma. The food is often quite delicious, but sanitary precautions are dubious. If you must eat this way, spend a few minutes watching the lady who is cooking and serving, especially paying attention to how she washes the dishes and her own hands. I've eaten at such places with friends who bring their own plates and utensils. For dishes such as *pozole, birria,* and other indigenous soups, makeshift stands are preferred by Mexicans themselves over restaurants.
- **Taco Stands:** One friend recommends that we bypass any taco stand that does not have a crowd of stray dogs hanging around it. That's his opinion. It's tough for me to pass by any taco stand without indulging. If you see people eating at a stand who "look" like they would not accept unsanitary cooking, perhaps it's the place to try.

If there were one "don't miss" place in all of Mexico, it is La Opera Bar on Avenida Cinco de Mayo 14, near Bellas Artes. La Opera used to be an all-male hangout. A typical dialogue between a wife and her late-arriving husband, would be:

"You're late! Where were you?"

"Oh, I went to the opera."

La Opera's neo-baroque decor, fine woodwork, moderate-priced food, serenading guitarists, and of course the drinking and revelry, make it a total experience. You pay the mariachis only if you request a song. Nearby, enjoy Mexican gothic dining at cafe de Tacuba.

Tips for Healthy Eating at Home

Tortillas are simply heated up on the oven burners, although they can be lightly-fried as well.

- *Pico de gallo* is the standard hot sauce, prepared by dicing green *serrano* chilis, onion, tomato, and cilantro, with a touch of garlic as a tasty option.

- *Quesadillas* may be prepared by placing either Chihuahua or Oaxaca pasteurized cheese inside a tortilla in a frying pan, and with just enough oil so that the tortilla won't stick to the pan, warm the tortilla until the cheese has melted; add pico de gallo sauce as you wish.

- *Guacamole* is made by dicing a large tomato, a half an onion, two small chili peppers, and cilantro, and then mixing with a mashed avocado. Squeeze a green lemon on the mix and keep the pit inside so that the avocado won't turn black as soon as it would otherwise. Serve with soft or toasted tortillas.

- *Frijoles de olla* (a type of bean soup boiled in a ceramic pot) may also be boiled in a standard cooking pot. Simply boil the pinto beans in water, with onion, a touch of garlic for flavor, and salt if you need it, until the beans are soft. The amount of bean broth is up to your own taste. Sprinkle cilantro and eat as a soup with soft tortillas and hot sauce.

- *Tortas* are prepared by slicing a crusty *bolillo* bread, sandwich-style, lightly frying the open faces of the bread in a minimum amount of oil, and filling with guacamole, the beans left over from your bean soup, sliced tomato, and cilantro (and a slice or two of ham or chicken if you are not a vegetarian).

Milk with coffee is often served at the evening *merienda*. Boil the milk, skim if you prefer. To a spoonful of instant coffee (decaf if you don't take caffeine), add just enough of the boiled milk to stir into a brown paste. Then add the rest of the milk and stir.

When preparing uncooked salads, make sure your leafy vegetables come from a reputable supermarket. Consult your neighbors. Mexicans use lemon juice as a disinfectant, obviously not a foolproof procedure.

If there were one single kitchen gadget indispensible to healthy eating and drinking in Mexico, it would be a blender. Mexican *licuados* (fresh fruit drinks in either boiled water or milk), and sometimes including mashed seeds or grains, are a nutritious and tasty alternative to the standard bottled soft drinks. *Horchata* is a tasty and healthy drink made with ground rice, cinnamon, sugar, and water. If ordering any of these drinks in a restaurant, make sure they are prepared "with purified water" (*con agua purificada*).

Mole is the only relatively complicated recipe I can manage. Half-cook/toast a portion of chicken. (Vegetarians may bypass this first step and use the *mole* sauce over enchiladas and/or bathe cooked rice in the mole sauce.) In a blender, place two cut tomatoes first, then a cut onion, and finally three teeth of garlic. After blending, fry the mix lightly in oil. Now add the prepared mole mix. (La Costeña is one recommended supermarket brand.) The mole mix already contains two varieties of dark hot peppers (ancho and pasilla), vegetable oil, sugar, sesame, onion, bread crumbs, cacao, peanut, and salt. Finish cooking the chicken in the mole which has been mixed with your blended and lightly-fried tomato, onion, and garlic. Add a slice of unsweetened dark chocolate to the mix as it is cooking.

Mexico abounds in fried foods and carnivorous dishes. There are many fine vegetarian restaurants, however, and from this brief annotated list of healthy home eating ideas, one can be sure that Mexico offers a profusion of vegetarian alternatives. Tortillas, pinto beans, avocados, cilantro, and chili peppers are a formidable nucleus for a vast array of creative and tasty dishes. An abundance of fruits from both temperate and tropical climates, as seen in the brilliant paintings of Tamayo, assure that Mexico is a paradise for those who choose to eat healthy.

Tips for Food Shopping

To alleviate the boredom of supermarket food shopping, take your own cloth shopping bag to a more personalized public market. Take a whiff of fresh and free enterprise. You may choose between several stalls for each product. Bargaining is permissible and expected. The produce is more pungent, tastier, and cheaper. Choose the best *marchantas* (market sales women) and once they get to know you, they'll offer you a little extra (*de pilón*), like the thirteenth piece of bread in a baker's dozen. Learn the question: *Qué me das de pilón?* (What little extra are you giving me?) Even the most confirmed anti-shopping fanatics will ask for their turn to do the food shopping when the venue is a Mexican public market.

SAFETY: THE MOST DANGEROUS GAME

I was gliding north by bus toward *El Norte*, having completed the final stage of my research for this book. Suddenly it occurred to me that I'd failed to get beyond the usual platitudes regarding personal safety. In light of Mexico's rising urban crime rates, I needed to devise a radical experiment for the last two cities of my journey: Chihuahua and Ciudad Juárez.

I looked at my *Pasaporte de Seguridad al Turista* (Passport for Tourist Safety) published by MasterCard and given away free at Mexican consulates. I read over the rules, things we all know like "Don't carry valuable objects or flashy adornments."

I decided to subject myself to a safety test. I would seek out the most dangerous neighborhoods of Chihuahua, a relatively tranquil city, and Juárez, known for its perilous streets. Both cities have been identified as stop-off points for drug traffickers.

I would expose myself to the most typical perils of personal safety and see what happened. The bus arrived at Chihuahua's Central Camionera on the outskirts of this city of 800,000. I hailed a taxi. "Please take me to a hotel in the most dangerous neighborhood."

"Why not a comfortable hotel near your dangerous neighborhood, señor? You could accomplish your goal from a safe location." From there, he advised me, I could at least walk to the neighborhood targeted in my experiment, that is if I was dumb enough to follow through on it.

But several important pieces of advice in my MasterCard document addressed hotel safety. To take a safe hotel and make brief forays into the danger zone would be tantamount to lack of commitment to my readers.

I had already broken MasterCard's first bit of advice: "Board only authorized taxis." Was my taxi authorized? I had not bothered to check.

The driver reluctantly dropped me off at an old hotel on a dark sidestreet five or six blocks southwest of the cathedral. Replacing the standard "goodbye" was a "you're on your own."

"Deposit important documents and objects of value in the safe deposit box of the hotel; don't leave them in your room," said the MasterCard safety instruction.

If I had requested a safe deposit box in this three-dollar fleabag hotel, the clerk would have broken out in laughter. When I got up to the room, I realized I'd found just what I wanted. I opened the type of door that even when locked, can be kicked open, just like in the movies.

The room was bare and dreary. The window looked out on an old alley. There was hot water in the bathroom and the bed was not uncomfortable for a three-dollar hotel. I left my passport in the room (one rule broken), and took my credit cards with me to the street (another MasterCard no-no). Furthermore, I had failed to write down on a separate piece of paper important data like passport and credit card numbers.

When going out, the tourist is only supposed to carry the amount of money needed for the excursion. I needed about 14 pesos, enough for two beers, but I took all of my money anyway.

"If you desire to go out at night, we suggest you contact excursions that are organized in groups. Consult the tourist service at your hotel," wrote MasterCard. What tourist service? I asked myself.

My hotel, of course, had never seen a tourist and specialized in one-hour visits of eroto-financial exchange. On the sidewalks outside,

I walked through beckoning streetwalkers. I decided that the honky-tonk bars might offer the greatest danger. I went into one of them, in the midst of mourning mariachis and a raucous crowd of seasoned drinkers. I slowly sipped a Corona, waiting for a brawl or a knife-wielding wino. Nothing happened but high-pitched conversation, complaints like "My wife doesn't understand me," or of graver consequences: "My wife understands me."

I left that bar and chose another, where the shouting reached the maximum decibel. I tried a different beer, I think it was Azteca, chatted with the grungy guys (there were no women except for a few barmaids), listened to the juke box, played a few songs myself, and left.

"Avoid walking on solitary streets," wrote MasterCard.

To break this rule, I set out for the marketplace, a few blocks away, the dingiest streets of Chihuahua but for suburban squatters neighborhoods near the outer industrial rings.

Nothing happened in the dark, empty market district either.

I returned to my hotel, suddenly realizing that in all these allegedly dangerous streets, I had not seen one cop! I was tempted for a brief moment to kick in the door instead of using my key. Once in my room, I discovered that all my possessions were intact.

The only precaution I took during the night was to cover the pillowcase with a clean undershirt. When I woke up in the morning, I realized that no affront to my security had occurred and my visit to Chihuahua had thus been a failure. I saw a few tourist sites and then left for Ciudad Juárez, a city allegedly more dangerous than Mexico City itself.

Once in Juárez (like Chihuahha a city of more than 800,000 inhabitants), I followed a similar strategy. But this time, rather than depending on the advice of a taxi driver, I asked a young middle class student where I could find a hotel in the most dangerous neighborhood. He pointed me in the direction of the back streets of downtown. "Watch your wallet," he said.

Bottom-of-the-barrel accommodation in Juárez consists of some dreary dives. Managers are reluctant to rent by the night when they can make more money charging by the hour.

I found a room for five bucks and went out into the night. The main drag, although labeled dangerous by my student advisor, looked too safe for my intentions. There were Texans from across the border looking for a little spice, and *cholos* (Mexican-American gang members with baggy zoot suits). In a few establishments, signs warned NO CHOLOS. The main Avenue Juárez seemed too mainstream.

I ventured off onto those sidestreets that were heralded as most perilous and chose what looked like the ugliest bar. The barmaid was about fifty years old, chubby, with a mean-looking face. Another Gringo sat at the bar next to a woman of the night, buying her drinks.

The barmaid invited me to *echar palo* with either of two prostitutes seated at the end of the bar. I told her that my wife was telepathic and would find out, so I'd prefer to have a Corona if her establishment permitted such minimal consumption.

She smiled, served me a Corona, and pointed up at the TV, where Televisa's eternal Ed Sullivan, Raúl Velásquez, was introducing the next guest on his Sunday variety show.

"They should put a condom over that guy's head," said the barmaid.

We chatted until I finished my beer. I left the bar and walked deeper into the darkest streets beyond downtown and when it became apparent that nothing was going to happen, returned to my hotel, where everything I had left was still there.

I had survived the most dangerous game, and came away wondering just how dangerous Mexico really was. I would be returning to Los Angeles, California and Washington, D.C., two great cities in the United States that are arguably more dangerous than Mexico City or Ciudad Juárez. How does one measure these things?

Similar experiments are not recommended, especially on crowded buses and metro trains in Mexico City, where pickpokets and *Panchitos* (youthful robbery teams) abound. I've known some victims of petty thievery but it's never happened to me. Sit near the door so you don't have to brush through so many people on your way out.

It is probably best that you follow MasterCard's advice regarding personal safety in Mexico. However, I've found that there is danger on both extremes. On the one hand, to disregard common sense safety measures like "Don't walk alone on dark streets in dangerous neighborhoods," could be a fatal mistake. On the other hand, I've found that tourists who are overly paranoid about personal safety seem more likely to stumble into trouble, as if they triggered a mechanism of self-fulfilling prophesy.

Mexico is not the most safety-conscious country, or simply does not have the economic means for maximum protection. One should expect to be surprised: by open manholes, donkeys leaping onto the highway, pitiful police shakedowns, delicious snack food decomposing under the sun at an unprotected stand. Mexicans expect things to go wrong and have a built-in precautionary sixth sense. People from more rule-oriented cultures come to Mexico unprepared for the unpredictable. If an accident happens, there won't be a litigious remedy. The best strategy is to exercise caution by expecting the unpredictable.

HEALTH

Preventive measures for personal safety may be more reliable than preventive health procedures. The fame of Moctezuma's Revenge is well-deserved.

Water and other potential enemies. Handl's *Water Music* was not inspired by Mexican drinking water. Traveller's diarrhoea (referred to as Moctezuma's Revenge and Turista) is by far the most common ailment for newcomers, and Mexican drinking water, whether the culprit or not, usually takes the rap.

Here are a few suggestions for preventing, and then treating this world-famous illness.

First and foremost, either buy bottled water labeled *purificada*, or boil drinking and tooth-brushing water. Boil water between 8 to 10 minutes; my own physician recommended five minutes, while another recommends 20. Ask yours. ·

After all is said and done, it may be unfair to lay all the blame on the water. At my university in upstate New York, African students got sick from the cafeteria food. The human body gets accustomed to a particular regimen of food and drink, and any change whatsoever may provoke diarrhoea.

In any Third World country, fresh fruits and uncooked vegetables, unpasteurized dairy products, and even fresh fish and meat may set off an adverse digestive effect in people whose systems are accustomed to processed and industrial foods. Mexicans use lemon as the all-purpose sterilizer, squeezing it on fresh salads. Unless you're in a five-star hotel, don't trust ice cubes in your drinks. Who knows what ancient beings might thaw out in your drink?

Before you leave your country of origin, consult your physician and take with you his/your preferred diarrhoea remedies. Some physicians (consult your own) recommend not taking medicines and winging it through the three or four days of a serious case, so that the body's natural forces can take charge. Fluid replacement, including potassium and sodium, is vital. Liquids such as weak tea, caffeine-free soft drinks, and pure water spiked with nutrients your doctor will recommend, accompanied by soda crackers or toast without butter is the traditional first stage of the recovery process.

Milder cases of *turista* may allow one to get out and continue with work or recreation. If this is the case, it is important to know in advance where the bathrooms are located. In general, plan to be near fast food restaurants or office buildings where you know there are accessible and clean bathrooms.

Tips

A catalog of other existing diseases in Mexico will unfairly suggest that you are in immediate danger. Mexico is a relatively safe country, especially at higher altitudes or within urban areas at any altitude. Here are a few tips:

- Use sunblock in the outdoors, especially at the higher altitudes where there is less atmosphere to filter out the UV rays.

- When needing any kind of injection, always demand a packaged, disposable needle. Lots of bad guys like hepatitis and AIDS are avoided in this way.

- Don't make brusk movements in the vicinity of stray dogs. Strays are usually harmless and are accustomed to the regular flow of pedestrians. Only sudden changes can provoke a fearful reaction that leads to a bite.

- Many medicines that require a prescription in more regimented countries are available over the counter in Mexico. BEFORE you travel and with the help of a health professional, make a list of those medicines which may be helpful to you. Mexican pharmacies usually carry a medicine directory attached to a chain on the counter. Whenever making a purchase, be sure to check the directory for side effects, even if you have a doctor's prescription. For years, I used an over-the-counter anti-diarrhoea pill called entero018formo, only to discover that the ill of its side-effects is greater than its immediate benefits.

- At high altitudes, don't spring into action immediately. Getting accustomed to Mexico's higher places is easy for most people, but it is best to increase intensity and volume of exercise gradually and to take profound rests and naps whenever lethargy sets in. After both positive and negative factors are considered, the net effect of high altitude to the health is positive. Many microbes and insects that cannot thrive above 2,000 meters, become nasty enemies in the tropics. The greatest enemy to one's health is the disease-carrying mosquito. To avoid mosquitos, lighter-colored clothing is a possible deterrent. So are long pants and sleeves, but in tropical heat, who wants to be covered up? Insect repellent and mosquito coils are good deterrents. In the case of repellents, there are various chemical formulas, and you should consult with your physician as to which formula is most appropriate. Then, in Mexico, simply read the label and identify the desired and undesired ingredients.

Doctors

As in all countries, there are good and not-so-good doctors in Mexico. I have appreciated my experiences with Mexican doctors, whom I found to be quite well-rounded in their interests. I've shared literature, chess, and philosophy with various family doctors. I've attended open medical forums at the university in Mexico City and felt challenged by the ethical and philosophical underpinnings of the seminars.

When it came to finding a doctor in a time of need, I depended on word-of-mouth. If it is still too early in your visit to have acquired a dependable social network, ask your local embassy to recommend a physician. The cost of health care in Mexico is relatively moderate. Ask American Express or your own insurance company about the kinds of travel insurance policies that will cover you for more expensive procedures.

Your local Mexican consulate, travel agent, or airline will advise you as to current requirements for preventative vaccines.

WHEN IT'S BROKE

When something mechanical is broken and ready for the junk heap, don't give up on it. Just as there is a cure for the body within Mexico's medical community, there are cures for broken- down TVs, automobiles, blenders, electric circuits, complex plumbing. There will be someone to do the job for a fair price. Check out the small workshops on your street or simply ask around. The repairman you need is probably right around the corner.

WHEN YOU'RE LOST

Getting lost resulted in some of the best moments of my life in Mexico. I've met such extraordinary people when asking for directions that I'm tempted to recommend the idea of getting lost. In general, Mexicans seem to relish the idea of helping you find your way. Asking for directions is a good way to practice Spanish in a practical way.

Dónde (where) is the key word. *Dónde está* (where is), *dónde hay* (where is there: *hay* pronounced AHEE), and *dónde se encuentra* (where does one find) are phrases that typically begin questions for directions.

STRATEGIC DIRECTORY

This practical directory is intended to facilitate and enrich your planning for and stay in Mexico. The utmost effort has been made to assure that addresses and phone/fax numbers are up to date, but given the nature of evolving telecommunications systems and the fragile tenure of contemporary business, it cannot be assured that every number and location will remain intact indefinitely.

For your convenience, categories in this directory are in alphabetical order. Abbreviations: T=telephone; F=fax. City codes listed in ( ) with combined city code/phone number always totaling eight digits. Access codes: Mexico *larga distancia* (long distance), 91; USA/Canada, 95; rest of world, 98.

For addresses, a five-digit zip code precedes the name of the city, on the next to last line. Underneath is the state. If mailing to Mexico from abroad, add the word Mexico (not included in addresses listed in this directory).

One can send faxes from offices designated Telégrafos or Fax Público. Rates are comparable to U.S. public fax facilities.

BUSINESS CONTACTS

The following are key contacts for foreigners who wish to start a business in Mexico.

Mexican Investment Board (MIB) New York Office (MIB)
Paseo de la Reforma 915 21 East 63rd Street, Main Floor
Lomas de Chapultepec New York, NY 10021
11000 México, D.F. T: (212) 821 0383
T: (5) 328 9929 F: (212) 826 6188
F: (5) 328 9930 or 202 7925 Hot line: (1-800)642-2434
E-mail: conmexny@quicklink.com

Banco Nacional de Comercio Exterior (BANCOMEXT)
(Mexican Bank for Foreign Trade)
Av. Camino a Santa Teresa 1679, piso 12, Ala Sur
Col. Jardines de Pedregal
01900, México, D.F.
T: (5) 327 6012 or 327 6000
F: (5) 652-9408
Note: BANCOMEXT TRADE COMMISSION OFFICES are also located in the largest U.S. and Canadian cities. Offices in Europe are located in London, Paris, Bonn, The Hague, Milan, and Madrid. Offices in Asia are found in Seoul, Hong Kong, Tokyo, Osaka, and Kuala Lumpur. Consult directories in those cities.

Nacional Financiera, S.N.C.
Insurgentes Sur 1971, piso 13, Torre IV
Col. Guadalupe Inn
01020, México, D.F.
T: (5) 661 4044
F: (5) 661 7296

For relocation or business property:
Century 21 México, S.A. de C.V. (Headquarters)
Monte Líbano No. 245
Lomas de Chapultepec
11000 México, D.F.
T: (5) 202-6777 or 202-8744
F: (5) 520-9227
There are at least 14 other local branches of the Century 21 real estate agency; headquarters will refer you to the branch nearest the city where you plan to relocate or do business.

For an Industrial Park Directory, contact BANCOMEXT.

For hands-on guidance, speak to the Commercial Attaché at the Mexican Embassy in your home country.

MAPS

Before you leave for Mexico, the nearest Mexican consulate in your home country will likely offer free maps available, or they may direct you to the nearest Mexican Government Tourist Office. One consulate gave me a comprehensive Guia Roji. Another provided me the Tourist Road Map México, published by the Secretaría de Turismo. Both are bilingual and include city maps as well as all the national highways.

If you are driving in Mexico and use Sanborn's auto insurance, you will receive detailed travelogs, also for free. Regional branches of the Mexican Government Tourist Office supply maps, and maintain representatives abroad in many U.S. and Canadian cities, as well as in Frankfurt, London, Madrid, Paris, and Rome. (See Mexican Government Tourist Office in your phone directory.)

PYRAMIDS AND RUINS

Selected pyramids listed by name of ruin, name of civilization, physical description, style, approximate time when built, other features, location.

Castillo de Teayo: Huasteca. Steep pyramid, 13 metres high, Toltec style. Stone sculptures. 1,000 AD. East coast, road off highway 180, south of Tuxpan, north of Poza Rica.

Chichén Itzá: Mayan. El Castillo is 24 metres high, plumed serpent sculpted along stairs, Toltec warriors carved in doorways at top. Pyramid depicts Mayan calendar, with 365 steps. During fall and spring equinoxes, the combination of light and shadows create the illusion of a creeping serpent. Within is another pyramid. From the top, view the whole site, ball court, temples, carved platforms, columns, other amazing structures. A short walk away, the Sacred Cenote, a huge natural well where bodies were thrown in human sacrifice. Late classic period, 600 to 900 AD. Recommended for all tropical ruin sites: stay over and appreciate ruins in early morning and late afternoon when the steamy weather cools down. Off route 180 east of Mérida, west of Valladolid. 2 1/2 hrs by bus from Mérida; less than 45 minutes by bus from Valladolid.

Cholula: The Pirámide Tepanapa, 60m high (largest of Latin America), is a metaphor of the Conquest, since it is grown over and a colonial church stands atop it. Access through tunnels. 10 km west of Puebla.

Cobá, Quintana Roo: A whole Mayan archeological city hidden in the jungle, thousands of structures, only a few restored, stone roads called sacbeob, remainders of frescos, and a 40-meter high pyramid called Nohoch Mul (120 steps get you to the top). Abandoned in A.D. 900 after three centuries of existence. West of Valladolid.

Comalcalco, Tabasco: Mayan, also until A.D. 900. Made of clay bricks rather than the usual stone, along with oyster shells. 50 km, an hour and a half by bus, from Villahermosa, and only 15 km north gets you to the Gulf coast.

El Tajín: Veracruz civilization, later occupied by the Totonacs, peaked in the second half of the first millennium. Unusual pyramid of square niches, stone mosaics, and many ball courts make this unique. Not far to the southwest from Poza Rica.

Monte Albán: An ancient Zapotec city on a hill, overlooks Oaxaca. The city endured for most of the first Millennuem. Tombs, ball court, murals, tunnels. No pyramid but you're already on top of the world when you get there and the site itself makes the ruins all the more impressive.

Palenque, Chiapas: Another Mayan jungle city with only a few dozen structures excavated, including a complex palace, frightful masks, and truly amazing carved reliefs. Only 69 steps to the top of the pyramid, but the leveled architecture and hieroglyphs are quite impressive. From the top is access to an interior tomb. The town of Palenque is about six kilometers from the ruins, and about 160 km from Villahermosa.

Teotihuacán: Only 50 km north of Mexico City, The Pyramid of the Sun dates back to A.D. 100, and is the third largest pyramid in the world, 248 steps high. From it you can look down on the impressive Pyramid of the Moon and the rest of the remains of the ancient city,

Photo: Carlos Mendoza

Ruins at Palenque

including a palace and parts of murals. If the jungle heat of the Mayan ruins is too much for you, Teotihuacán accompanies you with a fresh, temperate climate. I've returned a number of times, and never fail to be astonished.

Uxmal, Yucatán: Same Mayan classic period in the second half of the first Millenneum. Pyramid is about 40 meters high, with elaborate friezes. The whole site is stunning, with stone masks of the rain god Chac Mool just one of the incredible features. 80 km from Mérida, an hour and a half by bus.

Mexico is the home of many other pyramids and ruins, most of which can be located on standard maps. Whole books are written about sites like Palenque, Teotihuacán and Uxmal. Our brief descriptions merely serve as a menu for pre-Hispanic Mexico.

STUDY PROGRAMS

Many Mexican cities and towns have continuing education and university-level programs for Spanish language learning, arts, crafts, literature, anthropology, etc. Some of these programs offer room and board with a Mexican family, and may include excursions as part of their program.

College credit programs are sometimes directly linked to universities in your country of origin; you may obtain information and enrol directly from your home country. The source of information for such programs is the Department of Spanish or Department of Latin American Studies at universities in your country.

Moderately-priced continuing education courses, appealing to all ages, may be arranged for in advance. Many Mexican locations schedule even less expensive classes at their *Casa de la Cultura*.

This writer has participated in both credit and non-credit courses in Mexico and can testify that such study programs are an ideal way to immerse yourself in the culture.

Most cities with tourist appeal will offer such courses. Here are a few options with the best reputations.

Cuernavaca

One of the first cities specializing in continuing education for visitors, made famous by educational iconclast and priest, Ivan Illich.

Cemanahuac Educational Community
(anthropological slant)
T: (73)126419
F: (73)125418

Center for Bilingual Multicultural Studies
Apartado Postal 1520
62170 Cuernavaca
Morelos
T: (73)171087
F: (73)170533
(Active approach; no explanations in English)

Cuernavaca Language School
Apartado Postal 4-254
62430 Cuernavaca
Morelos
T: (73)154643

Instituto de Estudios de América Latina (IDEAL)
Apartado Postal 22-B
62191 Cuernavaca
Morelos
T: (73)170455
F: (73)175710

Instituto de Idiomas y Culturas Latino-Americanas
Apartado Postal 12771-1
62001 Cuernavaca
Morelos
F: (73)130157
(Courses for the whole family)

Centro de Intercanbio Bilingue y Cultural
F: (73)185209

Guadalajara

Centro de Estudios para Extranjeros
Universidad de Guadalajara
Apartado Postal 1-2130
44100 Guadalajara
Jalisco
T: (3) 653-6024
F: (3) 653-0040

Guanajuato

Centro de Idiomas, Universidad de Guanajuato
Lascuraín de Retana 5
36000 Guanajuato
Guanajuato
T: (473)27253
F: (473)22662

Instituto Falcón
Mexiamora 42
36000 Guanajuato
Guanajuato
T: (473) 23694

Mexico City

Centro de Enseñanza para Extranjeros, at the Universidad Nacional Autónoma, short, intensive Spanish classes, and other subjects related to Mexico.

CEPE
Apartado Postal 70-391
Ciudad Universitaria, Delegación Coyoacán
04510 Mexico, D.F.
T: (5)550-5172
F: (5)548-9939

Morelia

Centro Mexicano Internacional
Apartado Postal 56
58000 Morelia
Michoacán
T: (43)124596

Centro Cultural de Lenguas
F: (43)120589

Oaxaca

Instituto Cultural Oaxaca
Apartado Postal 340
68000 Oaxaca
Oaxaca
T: (951)53404

Puerto Vallarta

Universidad de Guadalajara Spanish Language School
Jesús Langarica 200
48300 Puerto Vallarta
Jalisco
T: (322)30043
F: (322)24419

Photo: Roberto Gaudelli

Puerto Vallarta seascape. A great place to learn Spanish, and sail.

San Miguel de Allende

Language and other courses, with specialty in the arts. Year round. Arts and writers' colony ambiance, cobblestone streets, colonial surroundings.

Instituto Allende
Ancha de San Antonio
37700 San Miguel de Allende
Guanajuato
F: (415) 20190

Escuela de Bellas Artes
Hernández Macías 75
37700 San Miguel de Allende
T: (415) 20289

Academia Hispanoamericana
Mesones 4
37700 San Miguel de Allende
Guanajuato
T: (415) 20349
F: (415) 22333

Taxco

Centro de Enseñanza para Extranjeros (CEPE)
Apartado Postal 70
40200 Taxco
Guerrero
F: (762)20124

CULTURAL QUIZ

A MOVEABLE FEAST

Ernest Hemingway called Paris a "moveable feast." That was in the 1920s. Today, the world's great moveable feast is Mexico. Yes, there are fine upscale French restaurants around the world, as there are Mexican restaurants. And when given the choice between drinking French or Mexican water, the vast majority of the world will choose the Perrier.

But French culture, even with its dynamic proletarian heritage, has trouble getting beyond the elite when transferred to other countries. Even the populist street life in movies with Philippe Noiret and Coluche or the Provence peasants played by Daniel Auteuil have not found the broad audiences they deserve outside of France. And try to find a street stand with French goodies equivalent to a taco stand, or an outdoor mural influenced by French artists.

With the superb Radio France International broadcast around the world, one would think that it would be easier to tote French culture from country to country. Yes we can find superb French wines around the world, but in raunchy neighborhood bars, you're more likely to find Cerveza Corona or Tequila Herradura than the Saint-Emillion wine that Hemingway so appreciated.

I have tried to transport the feast of France and the feast of Mexico (both of which I love) to other parts of the world; it is simply easier to transplant the joys of Mexico.

I try to cook French food, but the subtle dishes are too difficult and the bistrot steaks and potatoes don't interest me. On the other hand, I can whip up a guacamole by simply mashing an avocado and mixing it with diced tomato/onion/chile pepper, with the pungent *cilantro* making me an instant gourmet cook.

While Cezanne, Toulouse-Lautrec and Daumier are confined to salons, colorful street murals in the styles of Rivera, Orozco, Siqueiros, and Tamayo are found in many countries around the world. The Mexican Revolution and the demagogues who followed it made elite

Mariachis are found in many countries around the world, helping Mexico become a moveable feast. Hire them to serenade your loved one.

211

culture more accessible to the public arena, and gave popular culture a good name.

I would love to hear the music of Charles Aznavour and Edith Piaf on the same streets and in the same restaurants where I enjoy mariachis who dress and sing like Mexicans but come from other cultures.

In the international arena, Latin American literature has now eclipsed the European, with Mexican writers in the forefront. The stories of Juan Rulfo and Elena Poniatowska, the poetry of Octavio Paz, Rosario Castellanos, and Jaime Sabines, and the novels and essays of Carlos Fuentes have been translated into dozens of languages.

Mexico even invented a metaphor for a moveable feast, the novel *Like Water For Chocolate* (later made into a prizewinning movie), which is simultaneously a book of seductive recipes.

Ironically, the transmitters of this moveable feast include millions of Mexican immigrants, who, driven out of their country by poverty, and often scorned in the host countries they go to, bring with them their music, food, and zest for life. French farmers and workers either have a well-paying livelihood or are protected by a State social net; they have no reason to leave their country and become unconscious ambassadors of culture.

SITUATION ONE

You have a business lunch in a tropical Mexican city at a fancy outdoor restaurant. It is 35 degrees centigrade in the shade and the weather forecast predicts 95 percent humidity. What should you wear?

A Wear a suit and tie (male)/formal dress (female) and tough it out.

B Wear a long-sleeved, untucked, embroidered *guayabera* (if male) or a comfortable embroidered cotton dress (if female)

C Send an assistant to the meeting and let him/her handle the heat.

D Call your business associates and request to change the meeting to an air-conditioned restaurant.

Comments

In the Mexican tropics, informality predominates and the *guayabera* (male) or the cotton embroidered dress (female) is appropriate attire in business settings.

SITUATION TWO

Your car has spun into a drainage ditch at the side of the road after you've swerved to avoid a herd of burros.

A Walk or hitch a ride to the nearest town to search for a tow truck.

B Wait for the bilingual mechanics called Green Angels in their bright green trucks for free service.

C Abandon your car and give up driving altogether.

D Hail a passing truck, and then give the driver a tip for pulling you out with his handy rope.

Comments

If you walk to the nearest town (A), you may return to a vehicle without a radio or battery, or maybe with a missing tire. If the nearest town is only a few kilometers away, (A) becomes acceptable. Waiting for the Green Angels (B) is also acceptable, provided you have plenty of patience, since they pass by on the average only twice a day. The best answer is (D). In Mexico, asking strangers for help is a common occurrence, and truck drivers are still the guardians of the road.

SITUATION THREE

You are at a formal social gathering. How do you address the people you meet?

A Address people as Señor or Señora, with last name if you remember it.

B Address people by their titles whenever possible. The titles of *Licenciado, Ingeniero, Doctor* are respectively: university graduate and/or lawyer, engineer, doctor. Use the title with their last name if you remember it.

C Address people by their first name as soon as you learn it.

D Address people with the formal "you" (usted) as opposed to the familiar "you" (tú).

Comments

The best answer is (B). Indeed, if given a choice between memorizing a last name or a title, the title is more important. With (A) you are taking too many chances. To call a woman "señora" when she might be "señorita" could be taken badly, and to call a man "señor" when he might be "doctor" is also precarious. While addressing a person by first name (C) may be harmless, some people may be offended by the informality. A safe alternative if you do not know or have forgotten a person's title is to address him with the formal "you" (usted).

SITUATION FOUR

You find yourself at an important stage of a business process and are pressed for time. You must communicate with a new agency in the process.

A Phone the agency in question and ask if you can fax or mail the necessary documents.

B Phone the agency and ask for a personal appointment.
C Visit the agency unannounced so that you cannot be put off.
D Send a representative of your company in person.

Comments

In general, oral traditions in Mexico act in counterpoint with written culture. In the initial stage of a business process, personal contact accompanied by written documents tends to elicit a more rapid response than written communication alone. The time you save faxing a document to an agency that does not know you is minute-wise-hour-foolish. The best answer is (B). Answer (D) may be adequate depending on the level of importance of the procedure, so long as the person attending your needs associates your documents with a face. Once you are known within an agency/institution, electronic communication becomes more practical. Arriving unannounced is not incorrect, but you increase the likelihood of receiving a "Come back tomorrow por favor."

SITUATION FIVE

You are thrilled about a new business concept you have conceived and your enthusiasm has been corroborated by the fact that you have been included in a luncheon meeting with other entrepreneurs: potential partners from your business sector.

A During the lunch, be in no rush to elaborate on your idea.
B During the cocktails prior to lunch, initiate the discussion of your idea so that there will be ample time to convince your colleagues.
C If your business idea has not come up in the discussion by the main course, introduce it.
D Be prepared with handouts on your idea.

Comments

In general, the most significant social factor in conducting your business is to exude importance. To rush a discussion of your idea implies lack of confidence and lack of consideration for the social aspects of business. (B) is therefore the worst alternative. Since you have already been included in the luncheon because of your ideas, (C) is probably rushing it as well. Mexicans first want to feel socially comfortable with a potential business partner. Significant business deals take time and involve more than one get-together. (A) is thus the best answer; your patience will probably be interpreted as self-confidence. In case the subject of your idea fails to come up at all, handouts (D) may be considered a fair prelude to a second meeting. Your potential partners want to get to know you in a personal way first. Your ability to engage in possible conversational themes about family, *fútbol,* your impressions of Mexico, and your responses about the way of life in your country will engage your companions much more than the substance of a business proposal.

SITUATION SIX

You are invited to a social engagement but fear that your broken Spanish will be insufficient to communicate with the guests. You especially fear that you will become embarrassed when not under-standing what is said.

A Make an excuse and decline the invitation, and wait until you've greatly improved your Spanish before attending any social affair.

B Expect at least a few people to speak English at the gathering.

C Bring an interpreter.

D Attend the event and do the best you can speaking broken Spanish.

Comments

This is by far the easiest situation to resolve. Since you intend to stay in Mexico for a while, you are in an ideal situation to practice your Spanish. To decline the invitation would be to squander a great opportunity (A). To seek out English speakers (B) may be comforting but would also waste a chance to practice Spanish. Bringing an interpreter (C) would broadcast to everyone that you are not interested in learning their language. (D) is the obvious answer. In Mexico and other Latin American countries, most people greatly appreciate a visitor's efforts to practice Spanish, no matter how broken your Spanish may be. In a one-to-one conversation, you may request your companion to speak slowly *(más depacio, por favor–* slower please) and to please repeat *(repita por favor).*

FURTHER READING

No one's bibliography on Mexico could possibly include all the great literature from this extraordinary country. Here are a few good starters. For analysis of contemporary events, don't miss the syndicated columns of Carlos Fuentes and the *Guardian* articles of Phil Gunson.

Fuentes' first novel, *Where the Air is Clear*, is a cultural critique on urban Mexican life. His contemporary, Juan Rulfo, is among the most authentic portrayers of rural Mexico with his *The Burning Plane* (stories) and *Pedro Paramo* (novel). Rulfo stopped writing after these two slim mid-1950s volumes, but is considered by some as one the greatest writers in twentieth century literature.

I've read just about every book on the Mexican Revolution, but my favorite is John Reed's *Insurgent Mexico*. Reed actually rode with Pancho Villa, and no historian can duplicate this heroic journalism. John Womack's *Zapata* manages to tell a good story with fine writing even though it comes from academia. These two books motivated me to set off into the hills and interview veterans of the Mexican Revolution.

The cartoonist and social critic Rius is a one-of-a-kind artist, and the second greatest mistake of my life was to have not saved his old comic books, *Los Supermachos* and *Los Agachados*, which are available in libraries. If you like what The Simpsons have done in the realm of popular culture critique, you'll find the Rius comics extraordinary, and even more exquisite.

The contemporary magazine *Proceso* is no less profound than Rius, but lacks the sense of humor, compensating with superb investigative journalism. Also contemporary are the chronicles and novels of Elena Poniatowska, but I particularly enjoy her short stories.

Guillermo Bonfil Batalla's *Mexico Profundo* and Roger Bartra's *La Jaula de la Melancolia* are two of the best contemporary views on Mexican culture. *The Labyrinth* of Solitude by Octavio Paz preceded these two works and may be more poetic than objective, but it's a great read, and the guy won the Nobel Prize.

After reading Paz, go back four and a half centuries and enjoy Bernal Diaz del Castillo's *Historia Verdadera de la Conquista de la Nueva España*. Prescott's history of the conquest is the classic, and it's exciting to read, but Castillo was there when it happened. Less known internationally, Mexican historian Silvio Zavala is particularly insightful in disproving cliches about the period.

Any short bibliography on Mexico must contain an apology to so many truly engaging writers, both Mexican and foreign, who have written on the subject but could not be mentioned. And such a reading list must end with a tribute to the many brave Mexican journalists who were killed in the line of duty and whose murderers walk the streets with impunity.

THE AUTHOR

Mark Cramer and his wife Martha decided at one point in their high-pressured existence that their common joy involved living in different cultures. Before anyone coined the term "simplicity movement," they embarked on a path of radical downward mobility, discarding those consumer luxuries (and what some people would consider necessities) that had tied them down.

Rather than skip around the world and take photographic glimpses of great places to be left only with faint traces of nostalgia, they settle down in different countries where they establish roots and make lasting friendships. Mark's two books about the United States, *FunkyTowns USA* (1995), and *Culture Shock! California* (1997) have rare vision that could only come from one who sees his native country after having lived abroad.

Following *Culture Shock! Bolivia* (1996), Cramer began working on the present volume, making three return trips to Mexico, where he had previously studied, done business, and traveled extensively.

Mark Cramer holds a Ph.D in Latin American literature and history from the University of Illinois. He was well on the way to making a reputation for himself with scholarly publications but decided that there was more joy, earthiness, and social relevance in writing for a larger, but no less sophisticated, audience.

INDEX

accommodation 146–148, 150, 152
alcohol 107
altitude 44
Aztecs 14–16

bureaucrats 127
business contacts 200–201
business customs 121–133, 139
business practices 130–131, 138
business, setting up 131–132
business tips 130

Chamulas 58, 61–62
child laborers 82–83
conquistadors 20
corruption 163–169
Cortés, Hernán 15–17
cultural variance 40–41
currency 136, 181
customs checks 180

dares 106
Díaz, General Porfirio 25
dress 103
driving 65–68
    roadside assistance 67

economy 88
environmental protection 155–157
etiquette 102
exiles 85–87

feminism 78–80
fiestas 115–120
    calendar of events 115–120
flirting 105
folk art 62
food 66, 101, 110, 182–189
    eating at home 187–189
    restaurants 185
    shopping 189
    street food 183
    vegetarian 189
foreign companies 123–125
foreign relations 34
Fuentes, Carlos 73, 163, 165, 167

geography 42–51
    mountains 43
    places of interest 45–50
greetings 102, 113
Gringo culture 100

health 194–197
    doctors 197
    tips 196
    water 195
history 14–37
hitchhiking 65
hospitality 109–111
housing 181
human rights 58, 87
humor 18, 31–32

immigration 40, 88, 157
informal economy 83
insults 105

labor laws 137, 138
language 128–129, 171–178, 204
    conversation topics 178
    Mexicanisms 175–177
literature 20–22

macha-women 77
machismo 76–78, 94
maps 201
meals 101
media 71–73
meeting people 112
Mexican characters 52–98
Mexican Revolution 29, 53, 93
Mexico City 15, 37, 40, 46, 59, 69,
    88, 102, 109, 138, 149
mezcal 107–108
music 93

NAFTA (North American Free
    Trade Act) 89, 134, 137, 139
names and titles 103–104
    nicknames 104

Paz, Octavio 11
personal contact 127
personal safety 190–194
police 69–71
    corruption 69–70
politics 30
PRD (Partido de la Revolución
    Democrática) 36
PRI (Partido Revolucionario
    Institucional) 30, 33, 37, 40,
    61, 163, 166

punctuality 102, 150
pyramids and ruins 201204

religion 19–20, 29, 61
    evangelism 61
renting an apartment 146–152
road travel 43
rural-urban differences 113

Santa Anna, Antonio de 23
sex industry 73–75
sexual harrassment 105
social customs 101–114, 120
social gatherings 102
Spaniards 14–16, 19, 20, 22
stereotypes 9–12, 41–42
study programs 204–209
Superbarrios 90–92

tariffs and duties 134–136
tax system 135–138
tequila 106–108
Tlatelolco massacre 34
tourist card 180
transportation 182
    air travel 182
train travel 141, 144–145, 182
Trotsky, Leon 85

Villa, Francisco "Pancho" 26, 27,
    53–57
visas 180

war of independence 22

Zapata, Emiliano 26
Zapatistas 36–37, 54, 61–63, 80,
    96–98
Zedillo, Ernesto 164